The ABCs of Transformation

Using the Power Of Intention To Create A Better You And Better Future.

Kendall Williams

The ABC's of Transformation

Using the Power Of Intention To Create A Better You And Better Future

© March 2024

By Kendall Williams

Published in the United States of America

by

www.cb-publishing.com

All Scripture taken from the Holy Bible, quotations marked (NIV) New International Version®, NIV®. Copyright © 1973, 1978, 1984, 2011 by Biblica, Inc.™ Used by permission of Zondervan. All rights reserved worldwide. www.zondervan.com

All rights reserved under International Copyright Law. Contents and/or cover may not be reproduced, distributed, or transmitted in any form or by any means or stored in a database or retrieval system, without the prior written consent of the publisher and/or authors.

ISBN: 978-1-945377-34-1

First Edition Printing

Printed in the United States of America

March 2024

Table of Contents

Creating Winning Habits Through the Power of Intention	1
Introduction	7
A: I have the Attitude of a champion	17
B: I Believe in myself and my abilities	29
C: I have the Courage to be something more than average	45
D: I am Disciplined to finish what I start	55
E: I give a continuous, sustained Effort	61
F: I have Faith in the Lord God almighty, my creator, my sustainer	67
G: I understand that Good is the enemy of Great	73
H: I have created Healthy and meaningful Habits	77
I: Integrity is important to me	87
J: I am not subject to the Judgment of others	93
K: I am Kind to everyone	99
L: I Love the Lord my God with all my heart and my neighbor as myself	103
M: I have an incredible unlimited Mind	109
N: I will Never, Never, Never quit	115
O: I see only the Objective. Obstacles must give way	119
P: I am Passionate about this life and the way that I live it	129
Q: I understand there are times when I need to be Quiet	135
R: I am Resilient in my pursuit of continuous improvement	141
S: I am a Servant to others	147
T: I am Truthful with myself and others	151
U: I am Understanding that there are differences among us	155

V: Victory is mine	161
W: I have an unshakeable Will to survive and to succeed	167
X: I am eXtremely grateful for the precious gift of life	171
Y: I am Young at heart	179
Z: I live life with Zeal	185
Conclusion	189
About the Author	193

Creating Winning Habits Through the Power of Intention

I dedicate this writing to my children, Slade and Addyson, whom I love with all of my heart. It is my desire that the words that follow will serve as a guide to happy and successful living for each of you. Implementation of these ideas into your daily life through habit and intention will prove beneficial.

There are no hidden secrets or voodoo magic incorporated in these words, only proven techniques, thoughts and beliefs that will enrich your life. I know this to be true through much research and many trials and errors in my own life. Trials and errors are usually not pleasant, but they sure prove to be great teachers.

Understand that every person faces adversity, whether physical, mental, spiritual, emotional……the list goes on. No one is immune. Rich, poor, young, old, good, bad, large and small alike are susceptible to adversity. Just as fall follows summer, summer follows spring, spring follows winter and winter follows fall, there will be seasons of comforts and discomforts or challenges in every person's life.

The purpose of this writing is to help you weather the storms of life through each season that comes your way by encouraging a life of purpose and meaning, which makes overcoming these challenges much more manageable and meaningful.

To suggest that meaning can be found in adversity may seem odd or unrealistic, but indeed, it is the very place where it is found. How could something good come from something bad, one might ask. Just as fire removes the impurities of slag from steel, thus making it stronger, or wind stretching the fibers of a tree, thus keeping it standing tall, so it is with human life.

The fires of adversity and winds of uncertainty can serve to remove the impurities or weakness of an individual and are necessary for purification and growth if we accept them as such experiences. The key word is "if". Each walk through the fire or encounter with the winds of uncertainty provides us with an opportunity to strengthen the soul and validate the will or it serves to melt away an individual depending on how the individual responds. A proper response requires proper thought.

In order to have purpose and meaning, one must be equipped with right thinking and self-determined action. The self-determined person lives intentionally by choosing for themselves the attributes that make them who they are. Before a crisis or challenge ever occurs, they are prepared with an appropriate and effective response because each response is consistent with the attributes they have intentionally chosen for themselves. Each of these attributes works together to create a synergistic individual where the whole individual is much more than the sum of the parts.

Certainly, not every situation can be predetermined, just as not every response can be predetermined. However, developing a pattern of consistent positive responses to "small" challenges in preparation for dealing with more serious matters is important. Therefore, look upon each challenge as a stepping stone toward a future that is suitable to you and those that you care about by way of your response. Practice positive responses. Look at each challenge as an opportunity rather than an obstacle. Develop proper thought patterns (habits) along with predetermined personal characteristics to turn what would be considered a negative experience for the average individual into an opportunity to grow and advance toward the purposeful individual that you were created to be. The better you develop this skill, the more successful you will be in whatever endeavor you pursue. In other words, **before you can do something, you must be something!**

Begin now to choose for yourself who and what you are. Each individual decides for themselves whether they will be dependent on themselves or become a victim, submissive to circumstance or the whims of other people or organizations. **Know and understand this: you hold the pen that writes the story of your life, not the government, not the economy, not your employer, not friends or family, not anyone or any circumstance that should arise.** You and you alone are totally responsible for the story your life will tell so make sure it will be a story that you will be proud of and others will be happy to be a part of.

There are no secrets to success, nor are there any shortcuts. Men and women from the beginning of time until now have found success in many endeavors. Their success did not just magically appear. It became manifest through proper preparation, right thinking, and action. There is no such thing as an overnight success. A seed must be planted before reaping a meaningful harvest. There is no such thing as luck. Luck is when preparation meets opportunity, so prepare daily for what you want so that when the opportunity comes knocking, you can open the door and invite it in.

Just as the farmer prepares the soil, plants the seed, fertilizes the plants, and removes the weeds from the field in preparation for a bountiful harvest, you must plant seeds of good thought and action, nourish the planting with belief, faith, and positive mental attitude and remove the weeds by steering clear of people or places of trouble as well as removing from your life anything that will not move you toward the goals you set for yourself whether it be a physical or mental vice or obstacle.

A good farmer takes precautions to do everything within their power to produce a good crop and then turns it over to the creator to provide the harvest. The farmer is the planter; God is the grower. And so it is with you. Do everything you can to plant, nourish, and cultivate the greatness inside of you and allow the creator to produce a bountiful harvest through you. Let it go and let God do his thing.

To strive for greatness is something to be desired, not for fame or fortune, recognition or riches, but simply fulfilling the purpose for which you were created. God created everyone to fulfill a particular purpose along with a desire that each of us should flourish. Very few ever fulfill their purpose, nor do they flourish as he desires either as a result of lack of understanding, selfishness, misguided thoughts, careless action or lack of action. You were created for greatness.

All throughout his creation are examples of his desire for the creation to flourish. A natural disaster such as a volcano can snuff out all signs of life until seeds are scattered and begin to sprout. The seeds were already there, waiting to sprout and flourish, fulfilling the creator's designed purpose and plan for their existence. Plants begin to grow, turning a barren landscape into a plush garden of life, even more plush than the life that existed before. There are plenty of people who are volcanos, seeking to take advantage of and or destroy others. Be the one who leaves a mark on the world and paves a brighter future for those who come behind you, for there is no greater calling than to be all that you can be. Be the seed that turns an otherwise barren world into a lush garden of life. Just like the plant seed, you were designed to flourish and make an otherwise barren landscape a lush, thriving environment.

Choose for yourself who and what you will be and remember, **_before you can do something, you must be something._** If you do not choose intentionally for yourself, there are plenty of people who will be glad to choose for you and one thing is certain: their choices for you will be made to serve them. Be assured that no other person has your best interest in mind as much as you do. Choose for yourself and know the intentions behind the choice.

This is not to say to pay no attention to parents or other people in your inner circle who love you and have your best interest in mind. Learn to be a good judge of who those people are and a good evaluator of advice or information.

I wish I could tell you that I have done everything the right way for the benefit of myself and others, but I cannot. However, I am qualified to point you in the right direction not only because I have experienced great success but also because I have experienced countless failures. Both success and failure will seek to serve as success is validated by continuous improvement, which should be a priority, and failure will keep you humble and hopefully motivate you to make improvements.

Throughout the book, I share many personal experiences. I wish to point out that my purpose for sharing these experiences is not to glorify myself or to beat myself up over mistakes I have made. These personal experiences are intended to illustrate to the reader how a flawed individual such as myself (as well as you and every other human being) can choose to make dramatic, positive, personal improvements through the power of intention. As the only creatures known to exist with the gift of intellect, you and I have the power to reason and choose for ourselves who and what we are, thus what we get out of life. One of the most beneficial things an individual can do is to actively and intentionally seek wisdom. One thing is for sure: you will receive what you actively and intentionally seek. You will find in life what you are looking for. Speaking of wisdom, don't let this little jewel wisdom get past your attention and understanding. Read it again and submit it to memory; you will find in life what you are looking for.

Remember that there is no finish line. It would be wonderful to always "live up" 100% to the attributes described here, but there is always room for improvement. As Les Brown says, "When you shoot for the moon and miss, you land among the stars, so let the process begin."

Introduction

When I was a child, my family and I attended a church that had a small stream running beside the church building. After Sunday services, my friends and I would rush through the large double-door opening of the sanctuary and make our way quickly toward the small stream. On the way toward the stream, we would each select a stick or any other item that appeared to have bouncy qualities. As we made our way to the edge of the stream, we would simultaneously toss the sticks into the water and run down to the small bridge to eagerly await the arrival of the sticks to see who was the winner of the stick race that day. If we were lucky, we would have time for another race or two before our parents pulled us away, threatening bodily harm for getting mud on our "Sunday" clothes.

On occasion, one of the sticks would get caught on a piece of debris and the water would overflow the stick, pushing it beneath the surface of the water, never to be seen again. Sometimes, a stick would strike the bank on one side of the stream, causing it to spin around and around, ultimately striking the opposite bank and repeating this "back and forth" process down the stream. Back and forth down the stream from one side to the other, the stick would meet one obstacle after another as it struggled to make its way down the stream.

Most of the sticks, however, would catch the flow of the stream. Side by side or one right in front of the other, the sticks would gather together to "go with the flow," steadily making their way down the stream past the bridge headed somewhere, who knew where.

I cannot tell you how many times as an adult I have thought about the activity of the "stick race" and pondered how comparable it is to life. If we are not careful, we are oftentimes buried underneath the circumstances of life because we react rather than respond. We have not taken the time to invest in ourselves by determining who and what we are thus limiting our response mechanism. We are not prepared to meet the challenge of the moment. Other times we struggle to make our way through life, bouncing off one obstacle after another, awkwardly making our way through life. Most often, however, if we are not careful, we find ourselves going with the flow, headed somewhere for some reason most of the time not knowing where we are headed or why. If I am honest, I have found myself participating in this activity, which is at best unproductive and at worst dangerous or sometimes fatal.

To be the best and to get the most from life, one must be disciplined to avoid this type of activity. At all costs, steer clear from the temptation to go with the flow, aimlessly following others along the path of obscure uncertainty, as you will find easy to do and certainly encouraged by others. You may even find yourself ridiculed for refusing to go with the flow. People going through life without purpose or cause are most happy and willing to have you accompany them so they can have a partner share in the misery, as misery loves company.

Instead of going with the flow, blaze your own path, make your own mark upon this world, and help others do the same. It will not be easy to do, but the result will be a happy and fulfilled life for not only you but also for those around you. The influence of such living may appear to be minuscule, but do not lose sight of the importance of such a life.

A small stone cast into a vast ocean has no visual effect on the depth of the ocean, but one can be certain intellectually that the depth of the ocean has indeed changed due to the displacement of water volumetrically equal to the area of the stone. It is the same with your actions and attitudes. Each right thought, action or attitude "stone" that you cast into a vast world may have no visual effect, but be assured that each stone positively or negatively influences the level of humankind. Ultimately, the world is a better place or worse place for you and others according to the "stones" you have cast.

Always live with the end in mind. Each decision or action should be preceded by *conscious* thought. Thoughts that question the validity and consequences of action. Thoughts that develop our response mechanism. Questions such as "Does this move me towards that which is favorable to me and others?" "Does this adversely affect anyone?" "Would I be comfortable if others were aware of this?".

Thoughts are the beginning of anything that ever was or ever will be. Before your favorite chair was produced for your sitting pleasure, it was a thought in the mind of its designer. Before your favorite vehicle ever rolled off the assembly line, it was a thought in the mind of the design engineer. Simply put, thoughts are things.

The thought comes before activity; activity produces habit, habit produces character, and character produces results.

Thoughts > Activity > Habit > Character = Results

Keep this formula in mind and make it a priority to choose desirable thoughts that will ultimately produce desirable results. Prosperous thoughts produce prosperous results. Thoughts of lack and limitation produce lack and limitation. Guard your thoughts with your life as your life depends on it.

As a man thinketh in his heart, so is he. Proverbs 23:7

Activity is what turns thoughts into reality. It is one thing to think about and have good intentions, but it is yet another to take action. The road to failure and poverty is paved with good intentions, so be sure to implement your good thoughts and intentions by taking action. Sometimes, action is difficult due to fear of failure, fear of what others will think and even fear of success, but just like with anything else, do the thing you fear and the death of fear is certain. Without action, there is no accomplishment. Thoughts meet their fate at the feet of inaction.

Let him who would move the world first move himself. Socrates

Habits are born through repetitive action. It is believed that most habits are developed in 21 days; therefore, *consciously* repeating an action will produce the desired result for 21 days, and the action will become a *subconscious* habit. In other words, you will no longer have to put conscious thought towards it. I am not a Neuroscientist, but through experience and research, I can confirm that each repetitive action over time produces habit. Take, for instance, a musician. Every great musician spent countless hours of repetitive action to master their trade.

Anyone who has ever watched a talented musician perform can appreciate the development of such skill. Whether or not you like the song "Thunderstruck" by rock band AC/DC, you can appreciate the performance of lead guitarist Angus Young as he effortlessly hits every string and places every finger in perfect position, with perfect timing to create the rift that is so well known. It is absolutely mesmerizing to see such a performance of perfection as he effortlessly shreds the guitar.

One can only imagine the time and countless actions of playing that it took Angus Young from the first time he picked up a guitar until he perfected the rift and many others to become a true professional guitarist. Repetitive action over time became such a habit that he could probably play "Thunderstruck" in his sleep.

So it is with you. Create the right thoughts, add action to those thoughts, repeat those actions and over time, before you know it, you will have mastered that which you desire by creating for yourself a habit.

A good illustration of this would be tying your shoes. When you began to learn the process of tying your shoes, you consciously went through the activity of crossing the shoe strings, pulling the ends tight, looping one shoe string and looping the other string around the looped string. Next, open the loop and push another loop using the same string through the opening. Make both loops the desired size and tighten them by pulling the two loops simultaneously. You have successfully tied your shoes. Sounds loopy, but that is how you learned to do it 😊. Repetitive action over time created the habit of effortlessly and unconsciously tying your shoes.

Think back, if you can remember, how difficult it was to learn how to tie your shoes and fast forward to now. It is no longer an activity; it is a habit that is so ingrained into your subconscious, (no conscious thought required) you can perform the activity with your eyes closed in a matter of seconds.

And so it is with anything else. Identify the action(s) that will produce the desired results and repeat the action(s) until it becomes a habit, just like tying your shoes. In a matter of time, the actions are second nature, and you are on your way toward the desired result.

We are all creatures of habit, whether we realize it or not. Good habits produce good results. Bad habits produce bad results. Choose wisely for yourself this day the habits that will produce good results.

> *"We are what we repeatedly do; Excellence, therefore, is not an action but a habit." Aristotle*

Character is developed and improved through the development of good habits. Hopefully, by now, your character is developed such that you are aware of the importance of it and have made good character a priority. If this is not the case, continue toward developing through careful thought and repetition of perfect practice (habit) as this one attribute, ***character***, will define and determine the level of true success and degree of happiness.

Character is *who you are* when no one is looking. It is who you are on the inside, which is sometimes not always who others think you are based on what they see from your actions or the words they hear coming from your mouth. Character is the sum total of your thoughts, actions, and habits. Make it a point to match the inside with the outside. Be honest with the world and yourself by displaying the true **YOU** day in and day out.

It is critical that you pay special attention to the condition of your character. Be true to yourself and develop your character according to your specifications, not the specifications of someone else or some other group. The world still admires and appreciates people who possess genuine character and judges those with questionable character, even by those with questionable character.

> *"People of Character do the right thing even if no one else does, not because they think it will change the world but because they refuse to be changed by the world." Michael Josephson*

Results are the name of the game. Results are the outward expression of the inward character. Your success will be measured by the results you get. Results are measured by many different means in our society. To a salesperson, results are measured by sales; to a business owner, results are measured in profits; and to a farmer, results are measured by yield.

A large majority of society measures results in the accumulation of wealth. "He who finishes with the most toys, wins". It is quite appropriate to use measurements in the business world and it is admirable to desire wealth, but results in the business world and the bank account **alone** are not a true measure of wealth. There is much more to life than money and "things." Develop character by investing in things that stand the test of time and things that cannot be taken away. Understand the concept of "you can't take it with you."

> *"Do not lay up for yourselves treasures on earth, where moth and rust destroy and where thieves break in and steal, but lay up for yourselves treasures in heaven, where neither moth nor rust destroys and where thieves do not break in and steal. For where your treasure is, there your heart will be also."*
> *Matthew 6:19-21*

The fact of the matter is: this "stuff" that we believe we own is as temporary as the body that houses our souls. For a person who believes they are eternal beings (you are whether you think you are or you are not), "stuff" isn't nearly as important as the condition of the soul.

It would be sad to think about the measure of a person being limited to success in the business world and a fat bank account. As a matter of fact, a person who is interested **only** in business success and a fat bank account will not receive the results that pass the test of time. In the end, all the money in the world will not matter. You never see a U-Haul truck following a Hearst because indeed, you can't take it with you.

Business success and a fat bank account are a byproduct of genuine positive personal results. As mentioned above, results are the outward expression of the inward character. True results, those based on character, are results that pass the test of time untarnished by the wear and tear environment of this world and leave a legacy for those who follow, forging a path that others can follow toward a more fulfilling and purposeful existence.

This path is not an easy path, certainly not the path of least resistance, but the rewards at the end of the path have tremendous meaning and value as the captain of a mighty vessel on the high seas makes his way toward the safety of the harbor, "Steady as she goes" through one wave at a time.

> *"And let us not be weary in well doing: for in due season we shall reap if we faint not." Galatians 6:9*

Make no mistake. There is nothing wrong with having a desire to enjoy a healthy bank account and material possessions as long as it is not ***the primary*** objective of your life. In other words, do not sacrifice those special relationships in your life (God, family & friends) in pursuit of fame and fortune. Make it a priority to value special relationships and use material blessings to serve others. Put first things first and all other things will fall into place. Balance is the key to successful living.

Choose careful thoughts and take consistent action to develop healthy habits that develop genuine character and produce positive results for yourself and others. The following instruction is designed to do just that.

Decide for yourself this day who you are and what you are and remember, ***before you can do something, you must be something***. Don't let the world decide this for you. Make a concerted effort to decide this for yourself.

I have done this for myself, and the results have been amazing. Once again, I am not completely who and what I want to be, but I have determined the person I expect to become. I make progress on it every day as I move toward the summit of the mountain that I have decided to climb. As stated before, there is no finish line. We are all a work in progress, needing to become more than we are, stumbling along the way but always getting back up, learning from our mistakes, and making positive progress.

If you become the person described on the following pages, there is no limit to what you will accomplish. Feel free to develop your own ABCs. After all, no two of us are alike, so develop ABCs for Y O U.

The ABCs of Transformation are:

I have the Attitude of a champion

What a great place to start! Indeed, attitude determines altitude. A proper attitude is the foundation on which accomplishment is built. Any structural engineer will tell you that a strong foundation is critical for the success of a structural project. The success or lack thereof that you will experience in this life will be dependent on the foundation of a positive mental attitude that a successful life depends on.

We can be assured that we get out of life what we put in. The level of performance, no matter what the activity or task, is directly affected either positively or negatively by attitude. Attitude is the single most influential attribute, whether champion or chump. Consequently, it is absolutely necessary to be aware of the type and degree of attitude that you have at all times and make changes as needed to accomplish anything worthy of being associated with it.

Williams James, the father of modern-day psychology, once said, "*The greatest discovery of my life is that a person can change their life by changing the attitude of their mind.*" How in the world could William James, who lived in the late 19th and early 20th century, have discovered this principle all those years ago, and today, most individuals do not understand or practice this principle?

It is indeed baffling that we sometimes lose sight of the little things that make a big difference in our lives. Attitude is indeed the little thing that makes a big difference!

Be assured of two things as they pertain to an attitude that we must always keep in mind. First of all, there will be setbacks and challenges that will influence attitude *if we let them*. The fact is, life can be very difficult at times, so go ahead and expect the *opportunity* to deal with those challenges. Second, the attitude we accept for ourselves is a matter of choice. This choice is ours and ours alone. No person, event or circumstance can impose a particular attitude on us. We either choose an attitude that is beneficial to us or an attitude that prevents us from living life to the full.

Notice the words in italics, "*if we let them*" and "*opportunity*." We just discussed the fact that attitude is a choice. It is worth mentioning again because this is so important to understand and, more importantly, to control. You and you alone are responsible for your attitude and the results that follow, so begin now to take responsibility for both attitude and results.

A positive mental attitude becomes a habit when we learn to distinguish between reaction vs response to a particular situation. When we react to a particular circumstance, we are allowing the circumstance to control our actions, feelings, and emotions without a particular outcome. For example, a person pulls out in front of you in traffic, narrowly avoiding collision with your vehicle. A reaction to this circumstance would be to scream out a few choice words to the driver of the other vehicle, extend a greeting with the middle finger and speed away in frustration, not only endangering your life and those around you but also sending your mental attitude spiraling out of control, ultimately ruining your day.

Response, on the other hand, is a noun. To respond to something requires deliberate thought toward a specific result. In the case of the near-miss traffic event, a response would be focused on a specific desirable outcome, such as the safety of yourself and those around you and being grateful that everyone is safe, unharmed, and healthy and that no physical damage to your vehicle has occurred. Genuine gratitude changes an otherwise "bad" day to a good day, which was the deliberate, predetermined desire to begin with.

A great illustration of this point is the thermostat vs the thermometer. The primary purpose of the thermometer is to measure temperature. The measure simply records up or down based on the surrounding temperature. An attitude of reaction is always dependent on surrounding circumstances, temperature, if you will. The circumstance is the dictating input of the situation and the measure of our attitude towards it.

On the other hand, the thermostat measures the temperature and then takes decisive action to create the predetermined desired temperature input. Crank up the heat or cool your jets in accordance with your desired result. When a thermostat is set to a desired temperature, there is a constant application of heated or cooled air to get a consistent desired temperature. So it is with you. Set your *desired* thermostat and begin applying appropriate responses to any circumstances that will alter your desire and achieve the results you want. Be a thermostat, not a thermometer. As William James so eloquently stated, "Change your life by changing the attitude of your mind."

The circumstances of life will rule us *if we let them*. The choice to live under the circumstances, allowing someone or something else to dictate our attitude or not, is an important decision that all must make. Be assured of this: you are much more interested in your well-being than someone or something else, so you would be well served to be self-directed and in control, thus **choosing** the circumstances you desire rather than **accepting** whatever circumstances come your way.

This type of intentional behavior gives you complete control of yourself and the direction you have chosen for yourself while minimizing circumstances rather than living under the rule of circumstances. It is very simple. You are either controlled by circumstances or you are in control of yourself by using circumstances to make you stronger. A proper attitude turns circumstances into opportunity.

Remember, as was discussed earlier, there are those who find themselves faced with the same circumstances that you find yourself faced with, and they are most eager to share their negative thoughts and drag you further into self-pity and self-doubt. They are most happy to have you fall in behind them in what can become an uncontrollable tailspin headed toward a crash. Just like sticks floating in a stream, going with the flow, headed somewhere with no thought of direction. If you find yourself in that situation, jump out of the stream!

Don't fall for someone else's plan to "nowhere" for your life. Steer yourself far from the trouble makers, the naysayers and certainly do not keep company with those who see only what is wrong with the world they live in (their circumstances) rather than counting the blessings of life.

That doesn't mean that you should not listen to and accept valuable knowledge or direction from other more learned or experienced individuals. You should be willing to listen and accept direction from those you know are seeking to serve your best interests, such as a parent, sibling, spouse, or mentor, as well as those in positions of authority, such as a superior in the workplace.

What you choose *to do with this information or advice is up to you and the consequences of your action or inaction are **your** responsibility.* You are the captain of your ship and ultimately responsible for the direction and location of that ship at all times, whether wrecked on the reef, tethered safely in the harbor or sailing on the open seas to a destination called opportunity. The direction you choose to take with your life is yours and yours alone, and the degree of propulsion and direction of travel are factors of attitude. Allow a positive mental attitude to carry you swiftly toward the good that you desire.

The second word in italics is "*opportunity*." When undesirable and unexpected circumstances show up on our doorstep, and they will show up, we have an *opportunity* to **respond** appropriately or miss the *opportunity* and **react** inappropriately. From experience, I can tell you that I have missed many opportunities by accepting unexpected circumstances as an inconvenience or hassle rather than an opportunity, **reacting** rather than **responding**.

Reactions are usually brought about as the result of emotion. While it is important to gauge emotion, don't let it be the driver and certainly not the decision maker. An emotional decision is usually not a good decision. When you find yourself in an emotional state, allow the emotion time to "simmer down" a bit before an important decision is made. A proper intentional attitude will usually take precedence over emotion, especially when we consciously practice the habit of choosing attitude over emotion.

Worth mentioning again that there are two types of people in this world as it relates to circumstances of adversity. We are either thermostats or thermometers. An air conditioning unit thermostat is designed to control the air temperature based on input for a desired temperature. If the desired temperature is 70 degrees and the surrounding air temperature drops to 69 degrees, the thermostat sends an electronic signal to the heating device of the air conditioning unit, prompting it to respond by heating the air to the desired 70 degrees. A thermometer's primary function is to simply measure and display the air temperature.

A human thermometer is an individual who simply measures their environment (circumstances) and displays them for the world to see (usually with a level of emotion). Statements such as;

I can never get ahead

I get a headache every day

People are always so mean to me

Why does everything bad always happen to me

I am always broke

are the mantra of the human thermometer. The human thermometer is well-versed in measuring the bad things in their lives (circumstances) and telling the world their woes. I personally look back at times when I have been a thermometer and see a multitude of missed opportunities squandered away in the sea of woe.

Fortunately for me, I have been able to improve my life by improving the attitude of my mind, as William James instructed many years ago. I have done so by surrounding myself with positive people and choosing to intentionally practice a positive mental attitude. I "fall off the wagon" from time to time as most of us do, but my life is so much more enjoyable since I have learned to choose and practice an intentional positive attitude.

On the other hand, a human thermostat recognizes circumstances as they come along but uses a set of predetermined goals (a temperature setting) to change circumstances into opportunities. The focus is shifted from a circumstance, or set of circumstances, toward a specific goal or desire. As a result, we recognize the importance of attitude in moving toward our goals.

The successful stock broker recognizes a market downturn as an opportunity to invest in an undervalued stock based on his expertise and market research. A well-trained athlete uses a bad play as an opportunity to improve their skills rather than look upon themselves as a failure. A good teacher recognizes the opportunity to share core values with a student whose parents have taken little or no interest in a child rather than get bogged down in the circumstance of poor learning habits associated with a lack of direction. These successful individuals are able to see the big picture and the opportunity to change a life for the betterment of not only the child but the world, one student at a time.

Understand this: adversity is inevitable and necessary for the development and strength of character. We find this all throughout nature. The pounding of the surf on the reef is necessary for the reef to thrive. The vibrant life of the reef requires constant pushing and pulling from the tide. Without the pounding surf, the reef dies. The pushing and pulling of circumstances in our lives provides opportunities for growth and healthy living.

The mighty oak tree once endured being stretched and strengthened by the brisk winds necessary for its development. The constant back-and-forth tug from the breeze strengthened, strained, and stretched the fibers of the trunk and the root system of the tree, preparing it for stronger winds. The constant pressure from an outside source, the wind, strengthened every fiber of the tree, allowing it to stand tall as storm after storm tested its strength. Without this development, the smallest puff of wind would send the mighty oak crashing to the forest floor.

World-class athletes push their bodies and minds to the limit, enduring pain to strengthen and condition their bodies and minds for competition. No pain, no gain is the slogan of the athlete. Comfort and ease are a certain recipe for defeat to the athlete who requires the rigors of training to excel. Adversity is necessary for development and a person with a good attitude recognizes the opportunity of adversity.

> ***Good timber does not grow with ease. The stronger the wind, the stronger the trees.***

Adversity is inevitable and necessary for development. When faced with adversity, opportunity is set into motion through proper attitude. Attitude is the catalyst required to turn adversity into opportunity and make sweet lemonade out of sour lemons, so choose carefully the attitude that will move you toward the desired results when adversity shows up.

I love what Charles R. Swindoll says about attitude. I have no idea where it came from, but this quote from Mr. Swindoll was taped to the wall of my office, where it remains today;

"The longer I live, the more I realize the impact of attitude on life. Attitude, to me, is more important than facts. It is more important than the past, the education, the money, than circumstances, than failure, than successes, than what other people think or say or do. It is more important than appearance, giftedness or skill. It will make or break a company... a church... a home. The remarkable thing is we have a choice everyday regarding the attitude we will embrace for that day. We cannot change our past... we cannot change the fact that people will act in a certain way. We cannot change the inevitable. The only thing we can do is play on the one string we have, and that is our attitude. I am convinced that life is 10% what happens to me and 90% of how I react to it. And so it is with you... we are in charge of our Attitudes."

Having the attitude of a champion means that no matter what comes our way, we take it head-on with the belief that we will conquer all challenges. Champions expect to win. Champions expect good things to happen. Champions expect and understand that life is full of challenges while fully expecting to rise above the distractions that come along with the challenges. Champions choose to make lemonade out of lemons.

Without a doubt, life is an ebb and flow, a dichotomy, so to speak, made up of both good and bad experiences. Everyone experiences ups and downs. For someone to deny this fact is to deny the truth. The first step toward having the attitude of a champion is to realize, recognize, and accept that this is a part of life. Simply put, life is tough. Once you fully grasp this concept, the second and final step is to use a positive mental attitude to deal with it, as Mr. Swindoll charges in the quote above. It matters not what happens to you; it is how you respond to what happens to you that counts.

At this moment, I have a friend battling a terminal disease. Rather than sit back and give up or dwell on the terrible hand she has been dealt, she has chosen to confront the disease with a smile on her face and love in her heart. Her decision to choose a positive mental attitude, despite the terrible circumstances that she faces, not only has prolonged her life but has also dramatically positively affected those around her. Her warrior mentality is a blessing to others. Candace, you are amazing.

Ironically, while typing these words, a close childhood friend called me with terrible news. His pet scan results came back unfavorable. Just like Candace, he has been dealt a bad hand. Just like Candace, he already has a positive attitude regarding the news and will combat it with a warrior mentality. His life will be prolonged and those around him will prosper. My thoughts and emotions are all over the place at this moment while I think about these two friends. I truly admire how they have responded to their situation. They both understand that they are in competition with themselves in regards to their attitude. I can't help but wonder if I would be valiant and unselfish if I were to face these or similar circumstances. One thing is for sure. These two are my heroes. They are masters of attitude.

Motivational speaker and author Roger Crawford perfectly describes this type of attitude:

> *"Being challenged in life is inevitable, being defeated is optional." Roger Crawford*

One of the greatest examples of this is exemplified in the life experiences of Viktor Frankl, who spent years of horror in a Nazi death camp during World War II. Viktor Frankl endured misery and relentless torture at the hands of his captors. Many people around him, including his wife, did not survive the ordeal, yet he pressed on daily as those around him lost their lives as a result of malnutrition, physical and mental abuse. Despite the challenges that threatened his very survival, he found a way to stay focused on a positive mental attitude, defied the odds, survived the experience and wrote a tremendous book titled "Man's search for Meaning." I would encourage anyone and everyone to read this magnificent book. I would also caution anyone who picks up the book about the graphic and horrific events that are written about. When you finish the book, you will have a new outlook and appreciation of life. You will realize that the challenges you face are nothing compared to the challenges that Viktor Frankl and other Holocaust victims faced. You will come away with an attitude of gratitude for the wonderful life and the many blessings that you enjoy daily.

Do yourself a favor. Read "Man's search for Meaning". You will quickly realize how blessed you are.[1]

When I think about Viktor Frankl's tremendous grit and determination to not only develop and practice an attitude of survival but also find a way to share something positive that others could use from his experiences, I find myself absolutely ashamed of my attitude at times when faced with difficulties as I allow an attitude of "stinking-thinking take control of me by high jacking my thoughts which ultimately dictates my actions (or inactions) leading to poor results. These results or lack of results lead to more challenges, thus creating a vicious cycle if we are not careful. We must avoid this tailspin mentality and choose positive thoughts that bring about positive results.

So here is the bottom line where the rubber meets the road. Attitude determines altitude. We can either soar with the Eagles or beat our wings on the ground, believing that we are grounded in an existence of mediocrity, accepting what life gives rather than dictating the outcome ourselves. It is the little thing that makes a big difference. You and I have a choice between two different formulas;

Challenge…poor attitude…..stinkin' thinkin…negative thoughts……. negative actions or no action….more challenges = Defeat

---

[1] Frankl, Victor E., 1989, "Man's search for Meaning", Pocket Books Washington Square Press

Challenge…good attitude….clear thinking…positive decisive action = Victory

What will you choose? Will you choose victory or defeat? Do you have the Attitude of a Champion or the Attitude of a Chump? The choice is yours and mine to make.

Investigating the lives of successful people, we find a very striking fact: We find a common quality that is responsible for their success, which consists of a constructive state of mind. Psychologists term this constructive state of mind as a "successful attitude." Simple as it may seem, in most every case, the difference in success or failure is the ruling mental attitude.

The discovery of this remarkable fact by modern psychology probes to the very root of some deep practicable problems and indicates a way out of adversity and failure. In short, the positive mental attitude of the man who thinks he CAN, in contrast with the man who thinks he CAN'T, is practically the only difference between the one who succeeds and the one who fails.[2]

My father gave me very valuable and practical advice as a youngster when he would hear me say, "I can't do that." His response was always consistent and very simple; "Can't never could." As a youngster, I really didn't embrace the significance of this statement. As a matter of fact, my recollection on more than one occasion was that the advice was annoying, as is the case many times when wisdom is attempted to be imparted to an inexperienced youngster. Life's lessons dictate that some things must be fully experienced before they can be understood and appreciated.

Experience has fully vetted the accuracy of my father's advice. Indeed, can't never could. Just like the little train in the childhood story which was attempting to climb a steep hill repeated "I think I can, I think I can" in

---

2 Holliwell, Working with the Law (BN Publishing 2008), 108

order to successfully reach the summit, so it is in the "real world," a positive mental attitude is essential for reaching the summit of successful living.

Having the attitude of a champion does not just happen. Just like anything else in life, we must intentionally choose such an attitude and put effort toward the accomplishment of such a worthy ideal until the effort occurs so naturally that no conscious thought is required, at which point a habit has been formed.

Just like winning is a habit, so is losing. To be a champion or chump, the choice is yours. Choose (there's that word again) for yourself this day to have the attitude of a champion, enriching your life and the lives of those around you as a result……***Before you can do something, you must be something***. I have the Attitude of a Champion…..do you?

I Believe in myself and my abilities

When I was growing up, I was very fortunate to have parents who believed in me and often expressed their belief that I would one day be successful. Often times, as we gathered around the kitchen table for dinner, my parents would brag on us kids for the things we had accomplished and speak about our leadership abilities. At the time, I didn't think much about it other than being appreciative to hear positive encouragement from my parents. What I didn't realize was that each "kitchen table" encounter was another block in the foundation of positive growth. Each encounter instilled in us the value of "leaving our mark on the world" at an early age. It was the incubation period of the idea that if you do good things, good things will happen in your life. The values of citizenship, friendship, character, and industriousness, among many other topics, were discussed. As an adult with two children of my own, I long for the days of "kitchen table" discussions, which, for the most part, have become a thing of the past. I almost feel as though I have dropped the ball as a parent by not requiring that sacred time together we have allowed "life" to steal away.

These moments at the dinner table were indeed special moments. It played a critical role in the development of all of the Williams children. All of us developed a sufficient amount of self-esteem and self-worth to help guide us along the way. We believed that we had something good to contribute to the world, not in an arrogant way but in a dutiful way. I am very proud of the people that my two sisters have become and the families that they are a part of. The Williams kids are not perfect, but I believe our parents have reason to be proud of their kids. Their investment of love, sometimes tough love, and attention helped mold our character.

Many years later, as a rookie insurance agent, those kitchen table moments would pay huge dividends. One day, in a training session, I found myself partnered with an individual to perform "role play" selling. We were to take turns as the agent or customer, identify the customer's need and present the appropriate solution to meet that need. I started the role-play session as the agent and presented what I thought was a masterful presentation to my counterpart, who had a need. I was very confident that my presentation was excellent……until….. my partner began to dutifully tell me how pitiful it was. He indeed possessed a great vocabulary and used words I had hardly heard before to describe how bad my presentation was. He then said, "Let me show you how to do it." He indeed put on an impressive dog and pony show using his superior vocabulary. At that moment, I thought he was right. I actually doubted myself for a moment.

About a year later, we were all invited to the annual awards program. My partner with the superior vocabulary wasn't there as he had failed his duties as an insurance agent. As I sat there watching all of the big hitters stroll across the stage with a bit of envy in my heart, I heard my name called over the PA system. To my surprise and amazement, I was awarded the Rookie of the Year 2nd runner-up award. As I made my way to the stage to accept the award, I couldn't help but think about how those many positive moments around the kitchen table had paid off. I was reminded in that moment how important it is to believe in yourself, especially when the critics begin chirping about your lack of ability or their superiority. A genuine belief in yourself and your abilities will produce that "stick-toitiveness" to outlast the critics. When you believe in yourself, you are able to stick it out despite the critics or any other obstacle that might be in the way of your desire. Genuine belief in yourself helps develop self-esteem and self-worth, which are so critical to your success.

Self-esteem and self- worth are indeed extremely valuable tools to have in the tool box. These tools chip away at the doubts and fears that we all encounter but not all overcome. A strong belief in yourself and your abilities minimizes the effect of doubt and fear. Without this strong belief in yourself and your abilities, fear and doubt can absolutely destroy your hopes and dreams.

How strong is your belief system? Do you believe in yourself? Think about this for a moment. If you do not believe in yourself and your abilities, then who will? You know more about yourself than anyone else. Deep down in your heart, you know who and what you are. In order to live life to the fullest, experience it completely and reach your full potential, it is imperative that you believe in yourself and your abilities. If your answer to the question was "no," don't panic. We all have moments when we allow our doubts and fears to win the day. A day here and a day there is okay, but don't string together a week or month, which could turn into a year, a decade, or a lifetime. Many people have wasted the precious gift of life by allowing doubts and fears to win out over belief in one's self and abilities. If you answered "no," today is the day that you begin to right the wrong that exists in your life. Today is the day that belief in yourself and your abilities takes a front seat to any doubt or any fear that you have. Today is the day that you take control of your life and see the many good things begin to happen in your life. Today is the day that you have declared victory for yourself because you have intentionally declared yourself President and

CEO of YOU. You have replaced someone else's belittling belief about you or most importantly, your belittling belief about yourself. You understand that you are a child of God and your living small does not serve the world.

> *"Whether you believe you can or you can't, you're right."*
> *Henry Ford*

What a tremendously profound statement. Without a doubt, your belief system puts into motion the "results" process, which ultimately determines the type of life experience you will have. Failure results will be delivered promptly if you believe yourself to be a failure. But as you discard those thoughts of lack and limitation and replace them with thoughts of plenty, reinforced with a strong belief in yourself, you begin to see that no mountain is too high to climb as your belief system manifests things that were once thought of as impossible for you to do or have begin to pour into your life. Whether you think you can or you can't, you are right. As the old saying goes, "You can put that in your pipe and smoke it."

Success beliefs will deliver success; happy beliefs will deliver happiness; abundance beliefs will deliver abundance and so on. Your belief system is critical to determining the level of success and ultimately dictates a positive or negative life experience.

There is no better time than the present to think for a moment about your current state of belief. Give an honest evaluation about yourself on a scale of 1 to 10, with 1 being weak and 10 being strong, with the following questions:

Are the beliefs I have about myself most often positive or negative?

1   2   3   4   5   6   7   8   9   10

Negative   Positive

Do my beliefs most often propel me forward or hold me back?

1	2	3	4	5	6	7	8	9	10

Hold me back									Propel me forward

Do my beliefs about myself make me happy or sad?

1	2	3	4	5	6	7	8	9	10

Sad										Happy

Do I characterize my life as productive or unproductive?

1	2	3	4	5	6	7	8	9	10

Unproductive									Productive

Do I believe I am a leader or a follower?

1	2	3	4	5	6	7	8	9	10

Follower									Leader

Do I believe I am loved or unloved?

1	2	3	4	5	6	7	8	9	10

Unloved										Loved

Would I consider myself a happy person or a sad person?

1	2	3	4	5	6	7	8	9	10

Sad										Happy

When I am around other people, am I comfortable or uncomfortable?

1	2	3	4	5	6	7	8	9	10

Uncomfortable									Comfortable

Would the people who know me describe me as an encourager or a discourager?

1   2   3   4   5   6   7   8   9   10

Discourager   Encourager

When I think about my life, do I believe I have a purpose or am I here for no reason?

1   2   3   4   5   6   7   8   9   10

No reason   Purpose

Add your scores together. If you scored below 50, you need to begin now making it a priority to intentionally improve the beliefs that you have about yourself. Work diligently daily to improve your score by identifying your weaknesses and improving them. Just as importantly, identify your strengths and build on them.

No matter how low the score, do not be discouraged. Understand that as you begin to intentionally pay attention to and decidedly change your beliefs, you will quickly see results. As you begin to focus on the positive attributes that you indeed possess, all of the negative beliefs that you have held on to will gradually fade away. What you focus on expands. Stick to a daily routine of building up your "immunity to negative beliefs," and just as an antibiotic is a proven treatment for infection, "positivebeliefotic" is a treatment for negative beliefs and results.

When you catch yourself experiencing a negative thought about yourself, immediately replace it with a positive belief. I am not sure where I heard this, but researchers estimate that we have as many as 50,000 thoughts per day. To verify this, I did what everyone does: I Googled it. My Google search revealed that some estimates are more and some are less. No matter what the number is, we have a lot of thoughts in a day. Many of those thoughts are harmful and often lead to negative self-talk. For instance, when faced with a difficult task, we may find ourselves saying, "I can't do that." Stay away from self-talk expressions like:

I can't do that

He (she) doesn't like me

I never have enough money

I am not smart enough

I don't have any energy

Getting control of your thoughts and your self-talk will dramatically improve your belief in yourself, which is vital to a good quality of life and mental strength. To do this intentionally, make yourself consciously aware of your thoughts and self-talk. Keep an index card or note pad close by. When you become aware of negative self-talk, write the negative statement on the index card, cross it out and write beside it a positive statement more suitable for your belief system. This physical action will reinforce your awareness of thoughts and prove your ability to change your thoughts. Change your thoughts, change your results.

For example:

Negative self-talk	Replace with Positive self-talk.
I can't do that.	I can do anything that I set my mind to do.
He (she) doesn't like me.	I am a very likeable person.
I never have enough money.	I am able to pay my bills and often have money left over.
I am not smart enough.	I am getting smarter every day.
I don't have any energy.	I am energetic and vibrant.

Don't hit the panic button if your score is 0-50. While there is work to do, you have the ability to make significant improvements now that you know what you need to work on. Put your nose to the grindstone and grind. Build upon each success, celebrate, and be proud of every step of improvement that you make.

If your score is between 50-70, you are on your way. As mentioned above, practice positive thoughts and self-talk, and make it a goal to move into the next category. Daily intentional improvement will eventually lead to tremendous results, even on a small level.

If your score is between 80-100, you are doing well, but continue to work so as not to become complacent and certainly don't think of your score in an arrogant manner; rather, be thankful for the blessing of positive self-belief as you use it to the benefit of yourself and others. You have plenty of self-confidence and a healthy belief system. Again, even though you scored high, practice positive thoughts and self-talk and make sure to stay "grounded" in order not to become over confident or cocky. A quiet confidence will serve you well.

Once you have made an evaluation of your belief system and made proper adjustments to improve it by being a thermostat, ask yourself the following questions:

Am I building on my strengths and working to improve my weaknesses?

Do I believe that I have the ability to accomplish good things for myself, my family, my friends, and ultimately the world?

Do I use the abilities that I have to a high level or do I use just enough to get by?

If you are disappointed with your score or your answers to the above questions, don't sweat it. Instead, view this information as an opportunity to make improvements. The really good news is that you get to choose your beliefs for yourself. It doesn't matter where you are today. What matters is the steps you take today that will propel your score for a better tomorrow. With that being the case, be wise and choose positive beliefs that will generate positive results.

In 1980, I can remember sitting glued to the television along with my sister, watching the United States Olympic Hockey team take down the juggernaut Russian Olympic Hockey team. The epic win became known as "The Miracle on Ice" and later was depicted on theatre screens appropriately named the same. As a youngster, I had no idea the significance of the historical moment that had played out on the television screen before me.

The U.S. hockey team made up of college hockey players (at the time the U.S. would not allow professionals to participate in the Olympic games) was extremely out matched by the veteran Soviet team. The mismatch was validated just days before as the Soviet team destroyed the U.S. team 10-3 in an exhibition game. No one expected the rag-tag American team would make it far enough into competition to warrant a rematch with the Soviets, but they were ready to make history.[3]

Anyone who witnessed the event or watched the movie could never forget the American goalie Jim Craig made save after save from a relentless Soviet team, nor could they forget the tenacity of Craig's teammates who fought the battle of their lives on the ice that night. Coach Herb Brooks knew this was a special moment and told his players, "You're born to be a player. You're meant to be here. This moment is yours". Despite the giant before him, he believed in himself and his team, resonating with his team and leading to one of the greatest sports victories, if not the greatest, in history.

Simply believing in yourself and your abilities will help put you on a course to defeat the giants that stand or will stand before you. The concept may be simple, but make no mistake, it holds an unimaginable power. We don't win every battle against the giants in our lives, but a strong belief in ourselves and our abilities will lead to ultimate victory. Keep battling. Keep pushing forward the shield of belief that thwarts any attempts from naysayers or enemies to bring you down. Believe in yourself and your abilities.

---

3   Evans, Tony, 2013, "Kingdom Man", Tyndale House Publishers Inc

To believe in yourself is not an arrogant or selfish thing. To the contrary, if you don't believe in yourself, how could you possibly live life to the fullest and lead others to live life to that same destination? Whether you are a parent with the responsibility of leading your family or whether you are charged as the President of a multi-million dollar business to lead, neither can find success without believing in one's self and their abilities.

I might add that the responsibility for the parent is just as important if not more important than that of the president of a multi-million dollar business. The natural instinct is to believe that the President in this example is much more important simply because society holds this person in such high esteem. Since others are dependent on the decisions made by either and lives are shaped as a result of these decisions, a strong self-belief is critical for the success of each and the well-being of all.

The fact is you are important no matter what your area of responsibility is. What could be more honorable than being a good parent, a good teacher, a good friend, a good spouse, a good co-worker, or a good child? The fact is that you cannot be good at any of these or anything else if you do not believe in yourself.

Once again, this belief is not one of arrogance; it is one of confidence, and to enjoy it purposefully and to the fullest serves yourself and others. Your self-confidence is much needed in the world today to help guide others to greater heights and toward a better life. This belief and self-confidence will propel you as well as those around you, to experience winning as you journey on your way.

In my opinion and the opinion of many others, one of the greatest athletes that ever participated in any sport was Michael Jordan. Whether anyone was a Chicago Bulls fan or not, they had to love to watch Michael Jordan play basketball. Michael Jordan seemed to live for the moment when the game was on the line with one shot to win or loose. Every player or coach on the opposing team, every spectator in the arena or watching via television, every sports broadcaster, and everyone in the sports world knew that Michael Jordan would take the final shot. The question was not who was going to take the shot but from where would Jordan take the shot.

While Jordan didn't make every shot with the game on the line, he did make a lot of them. One thing is for sure. He wasn't afraid to take the shot while the entire world looked on. Why? Simply put, aside from the phenomenal athletic ability that Michael Jordan possessed, he also believed in himself and his abilities. As the world looked on, it never seemed he was fazed by the moment, whether big or small. It was as if he knew in his heart of hearts that if his team were going to win, he believed he was the one most likely to make the shot. I didn't watch all of the Bulls games back in the day and wasn't what I would call a big NBA fan, but I must admit I was impressed by Michael Jordan's seeming unshakeable belief in himself and his abilities.

I have never met or interviewed Jordan and haven't read much about him, but I feel quite certain from simply watching him play that his belief in himself and his abilities, in combination with his amazing abilities, were what propelled him to greatness. One without the other would have never resulted in such a magnificent display of achievement.

Certainly, there are not many world-class athletes who are worthy of lacing up Jordan's shoes, let alone being compared to him. He, without a doubt, was a special athletic creation with phenomenal athletic ability. As true as that may be, his accomplishments would have been insignificant based solely on his ability. Without belief in himself, Jordan would certainly never have taken the shots and been able to excel to the magnificent level that he reached.

So it is with you and I. No matter what degree of ability we are gifted by the creator, we must believe in ourselves and our abilities in order to live life to the fullest and be taken to heights that are otherwise impossible. We must take each shot with confidence. We must know at the end of the day, hit or miss, we believe in ourselves enough to take the shot.

While we cannot all be Michael Jordan or achieve the level of greatness that he was able to achieve in his public arena, we all have something to offer to this world: a purpose, a calling. We all have a legacy to leave. The sooner we begin to believe in ourselves and our abilities, the greater that legacy will be.

Each of us is gifted differently. You possess gifts that are unique to you. Perhaps you have discovered them or perhaps you have not. Perhaps you know what they are and believe that they are insignificant. If that is the case, do not buy into those beliefs. If George Washington had possessed this type of mentality, he would not have graced the pages of history books as the first President of the United States. If Albert Einstein had believed his teachers who told his parents that he was not good at mathematics, he would have never developed the theory of relativity that he is so well known for today.

Perhaps there are those around you who are telling you that you have no value or that you have no skills or contribution to the world. Perhaps you believe this hogwash. The fact is you have value and you have something to offer this world, so be about the business of believing in yourself and your abilities. Be about the business of contributing to the world and having a positive influence on those around you. After all, what someone else thinks about you is none of your business.

> *"What someone else thinks of me is none of my business."*
> *Eleanor Roosevelt*

Be aware that you, just like everyone else, have strengths and weaknesses. You were designed and equipped to excel at some things more so than others. Everyone cannot be a magnificent musician, a polished sales person, a well-renowned artist, or a professional athlete. Understand that it doesn't matter what our profession or activities are; what matters is that we do our best at whatever it is we do. Our job title should be "The best," no matter what it is we do. Your belief system will influence your ability to perform at a high level and be the best.

The best is not always the most financially lucrative or well-known, so understand that the best are not necessarily identified by riches or fame. There are successful people who have enjoyed riches or fame by being the best at something, but there are many other little-known people with a servant's heart who are successful because they placed character and reputation above wealth and riches.

History has proven that success has evaded some who have had extraordinary ability and opportunity, while others with average ability and little opportunity have climbed the mountain of success. One could conclude that success is not measured by what an individual accomplishes; success is measured by what an individual accomplishes based on the ability that the individual possesses.

If you haven't already done so, identify your strengths and weaknesses. Build on your strengths and improve on your weaknesses. Whatever you do, believe in yourself and your abilities. Focusing on strengths will boost your confidence in your abilities, and developing a weakness will provide the necessary personal growth required to excel as a human being. This activity will soon identify weaknesses as opportunities.

Be very careful not to dwell on another person's gift and wish it were yours. Chances are they are looking at you and wishing they had your gifts. This type of behavior not only opens the door for unhealthy, envious thoughts but also minimizes the importance of the abilities that you have. The results are detrimental to the enrichment of others and yourself, which is the exact opposite of what everyone should try to accomplish in the limited time that there is on this earth.

Believe in yourself and your abilities while at the same time celebrating the success of others. Envy and jealousy of another's success will certainly cause success to flee from you as a human would flee from a crazed animal wishing to harm them. There is no place for envy and jealousy in the life of a successful person. A person who cannot celebrate the success of another does not deserve success for themselves and most likely will not have it.

One must suppose that it is human nature to wish for something different from what one already possesses with the constant attempts to be or have something different from who we are and what we have. Perhaps you have heard it said, "the grass is always greener on the other side of the fence." Growing up on a cattle farm afforded me a first-hand look at this type of behavior. The grass on the outside of the fence obviously appeared to be much better than that inside the fence, based on the numerous attempts and successful escapes from the pasture to feed on the grass on the other side of the fence. Keep your head in your own pasture. It is, by the way, *your* pasture. If you don't take care of it, you can be assured that no one else will. Dream big in that pasture and be grateful for the grass that grows on your side of the fence.

> *"What the mind can conceive and <u>believe</u>, it can achieve." W. Clement Stone*

My parents often reminded me and my sisters as youngsters that we could be or do anything we wanted to be. While I do believe that gifts and abilities are certainly necessary, I also believe that when we believe in ourselves and our abilities, achievement is possible. Don't take my word for it. Dig up the archives of the NBA slam dunk contest and watch 5'6" Spud Webb win the contest or watch 5'9" Wes Welker make defensive backs in the NFL look silly. These two men may have been challenged by size compared to most professional athletes that they competed with, but they were giants on the court and field of competition.

Unfortunately, much of the talk about being able to do or be anything that we wanted to be from my parents went in one ear and out of the other, speaking for myself of course. At the time, it didn't register as something important that a youngster needed to concentrate on and as a result, I did live through periods of doubt; however, these words did stick enough to mask the moments of doubt and push me towards achievement.

My parents certainly knew that it was not registering, but fortunately for me, they never gave up. These words of encouragement continued to roll off of their lips despite my lack of attention or concern. Over all, this parental leadership has served me well, as this advice has brought success in many arenas of life. Whether family, social, business, spiritual, personal, or professional, all areas of my life have benefited from believing in myself and my abilities. While I certainly haven't always gotten it right, I have been able to get a lot closer than I otherwise would have.

What do you believe in? Who do you believe in? Do you believe in yourself? The fact is, as I have heard many times, "you will either believe in something or you will fall for anything". You must begin by believing in yourself and your abilities; otherwise, your life and your actions will mimic the beliefs that others have about you. If you have been taught that this is a sign of arrogance or over confidence, then you have been taught wrong. Granted there are those who are arrogant and over confident, but a deep-rooted belief in yourself is vital and it can be accomplished with humility.

The God of the universe gifted you with a unique skill set and abilities. God doesn't make junk, so be assured of your abilities and understand the importance and necessity for your success and the success of those around you is dependent on a strong belief system. **Before you can do something, you must be something.**

I believe in myself and my abilities……….. Do you?

I have the Courage to be something more than average

If we are not careful, we easily fall victim to negative self-worth based on the opinions of others. When we allow this to happen, we pattern our behavior based on the opinions of others about who or what we should be. Often times, this behavior is not in our best interest.

As described in the introduction of this book, we fall into a pattern of "going with the flow" because of our importance in "fitting in" with the crowd. We value the thoughts and expectations of others more than our own. We allow others' supposed evaluation of ourselves to take precedence over who and what we are rather than dictating for ourselves a conscious intentional "self-description" by ourselves. Peer pressure has us believe that it is just much easier to "be normal" when, in reality, the definition of what the world would say is "normal" changes on a daily basis, so why try to live up to the expectations of others?

The intentional person blazes their own trail despite what the "world" believes is best for them. They decide for themselves what is best for them and often times, it is not what the "world" believes is best. To do this takes courage.

Courage is perhaps one of the most honorable of human traits. To possess true grit and courage, one must be an exceptional human being, a human being who believes in themselves and pays little to no attention to what others think of them. When courage becomes an intentional characteristic, you will follow the convictions that match your purpose. Were it not for courage, a civilized, productive society would be non-existent and the many things that we enjoy would not be possible.

Courageous people respond to circumstances that do not match their ultimate belief or desire despite what others think. Courageous people have an overwhelming desire to do what is right for themselves and others. They are interested in the greater good of society. Cowards are only interested in themselves.

Many politicians fit the coward description by selling their soul through self-serving activity, self-preservation, self-promotion, and advancement of self rather than courageously doing what is right for the greater good. Despite the attempt to rewrite the narrative by themselves and a compliant media to reflect one's so-called service as "good and honorable," history will expose the cowards and separate them from the courageous. Honorable people know deep in their souls if they are courageous or cowardly. You may be able to fool the masses, but you cannot fool yourself.

It takes courage to be something more than average and you are destined to be and do more that "just getting by." The problem with being average is that there is nothing in sight to shoot for. In addition, the bar to be considered average seems to be lowered every year. There was a time when the average person possessed attributes like hard working, sober, respectful, independent, trustworthy and high moral values. It seems that the average person today wants a paycheck but don't want a job. The average person today will use anything from prescription drugs to battery acid to get high.

The average person today has respect for only themselves. The average person today will find any reason under the sun to get a Government check or receive a lawsuit settlement. The average person today cannot be trusted. The average person today isn't concerned about having personal values; they are only concerned about living for the moment. If it is good for ME, then it is good no matter how it affects others. The standard of average has steadily decreased in my lifetime.

There certainly are still plenty of good people in the world, and there are those who would argue that this is not a good description of the average person. I would admit that this is a pretty harsh description of the average person but if it is not a 100% accurate description, I don't think anyone could argue that we are headed in that direction fast. Whatever the average is, to strive to be better than average should be your goal. Can you imagine what a wonderful world this would be if everyone would strive to be better than average? Of course, the bar would be raised, but everyone would benefit.

Average people, as well as less than average people, will want you to be just like them and remain average. As a matter of fact, many of them will criticize you for trying to become something more than average. The rewards of life are intended for those who are willing to take risks for the betterment of their environment and the environment of those around them. Above-average people are more willing to take those risks because they have a great attitude and a strong belief system, both of which we have already discussed. They understand the concept: "nothing ventured, nothing gained" and "no risk, no reward." They are willing to bet on themselves because they have proven to themselves that they are worthy. Sometimes, the hardest sell is to sell yourself to yourself, which above-average people do consistently.

One of the biggest misconceptions in our world today is that "someone owes me," whether it is an individual, government, or company. Understand this: the world doesn't owe you anything. Let's repeat this again to make sure you do not miss it. The world does not owe you anything. Success comes to those who are willing to have the courage to seek out the desires of their heart and be willing to **earn** them through the exertion of time and effort. There is no such thing as a free lunch, education, or healthcare. Someone is paying for all of that "*free*" stuff. Success favors those who understand this fact and have the courage to be more than average.

The one who has the courage to become something more than average understands the concept of earning. This person understands that most anything worthwhile requires a generous effort. A good marriage requires a generous effort from both husband and wife as well as courage from both. Any professional skill requires a generous effort to develop the necessary skill level to be considered professional as well as the courage to devote the time and effort required. Being a good parent, employee, friend……_____; you fill in the blank, requires a generous effort. Being good at anything doesn't just happen. Rather than let life happen, make life happen for you by having the courage to be something more than average.

Would a deadbeat father deserve affection from his kids? Would an employee with a poor work ethic or attendance record deserve a raise? Of course, not though some would expect it anyway. The rewards in life are generally measured in proportion to the investment of thoughtful consideration and effort. The more that is put in, the more that is to be received. Put a little in, get a little back. Put a lot in, get a lot back. In simple terms, expect to reap what you sow.

Some would say that there is a price to pay for these things when, in reality, there is not price to pay. Instead, there is an investment with a return on the investment. A loving/responsible parent does not pay the price for being loving and responsible. They enjoy the benefits of being a loving/responsible parent. A person doesn't pay the price for being a hard worker; they enjoy the benefits of accomplishment and a healthy paycheck. A married couple does not pay the price for a good marriage; they enjoy the benefits of a good marriage and a happy, loving homelife.

There will certainly be those who will question this analysis by asking, "What about the loving/responsible parent who has the derelict child? What about the hard-working employee who never receives a raise and is treated unfairly by the employer? What about the spouse who is a model spouse and is asked for a divorce by their spouse?" In other words, why do bad things sometimes happen to good people? This is a question that can only be answered by our creator. Experience seems to indicate that though it is sometimes difficult to understand "why," all things happen for a reason. It may be for nothing more than personal growth as preparation for some future event where a steady hand or "cool and collected" demeanor would be critical to the outcome. For certain, there is always the opportunity for growth associated with adversity. This analysis is not intended to belittle a person who is struggling to deal with a tragic situation or event. If you find yourself in that category, by all means, seek professional help rather than bear the burden alone.

What makes the difference between a great leader and an average leader? What makes the difference between an average spouse or a great spouse, an average parent or a great parent? What makes one rush into the face of danger, whether in warfare, business, or personal issues and another fold like a tent? What makes one tackle adversity head-on while another sheepishly shies away? What makes one do the right thing when the right thing doesn't bring prosperous results or just simply is not a pleasant thing to do or while everyone else is doing just the opposite? Plain and simple, it is courage that makes one be something more than average.

Courage is hard to find in a world that encourages greed, hatred, and other selfish desires. When temptations of greed or hatred hold your attention, inhale a large breath of courage to do what you know is right in your heart and exhale the temptation from your presence. The world often encourages and promotes those who go with the flow, conform to the norm, and are politically correct. It encourages the selfish pursuit of things that render personal gain or benefit at the expense of others. It encourages the practice of hatred toward our fellow human beings.

Courage trumps these selfish desires. Courage stands boldly on the side of service. Ultimately, one with courage stands tall above the world as well as those whose focus is of a worldly nature and rewards the one with courage in their heart with respect and honor from others.

Courage is the cure for a corrupt world. Courage is the cure for a fearful heart. Courage is the medicine for weakness, the food of champions. It is almost certainly something possessed by every great leader throughout history. History will reveal the courageous as well as the self-proclaimed so-called "leaders" who are only concerned with power and money. Media outlets can spin stories of their greatness and hide their transgressions on humanity. They can attempt to rewrite history to promote relevance toward their agenda. They can spend all the money in the world to try to right a wrong, but in the end, history will reveal the courageous who selflessly walked by their own drumbeat, invisible because they are not trying to have the world fall in line yet visible and ultimately relevant because they had the courage to be something more than average by following what they know to be right in their heart, oftentimes what is not right in the eyes of the world.

Unfortunately, many people with tremendous abilities or platforms to exact positive change often fall victim to fear of what "others" might think. Fear dampens courage and discourages (the opposite of courage) us from taking a chance to become something more than average because if we fail, others will judge us. Dis-courage kicks in and off we go, living the life that someone else has determined is best for us, namely, best for them.

So, how would one overcome fear and replace it with courage? Plain and simple, just face fear head-on and do the thing that you know in your heart is right. Do the thing you fear and the death of fear is certain. When we repeatedly practice overcoming fear by proving to ourselves that there is nothing to fear by performing activities that bring about the emotion of fear, the emotion of fear will gradually fade away and ultimately disappear. Embrace courage and steer away from the disgrace or a cowardice lifestyle by doing what you know in your heart is right, even though it may not fit the pattern of the world.

While there are some things that are dangerous and we should respect them, most of our fears are never realized. For instance, most people have a healthy fear of snakes, yet there are those who are professional snake handlers whose work of "handling" snakes is important for things such as removal/relocation from a populated area or one who extracts venom for the purpose of anti-venom. They have experienced the dangerous activity of handling venomous snakes enough that they are able to do something that would terrify most people on a daily basis because they have practiced the dangerous activity enough that fear is either minimal or non-existent.

Do the thing you fear and the death of fear is certain.

In the classic movie *The Yellow Brick Road*, Lion found himself in a terrible predicament. Lion was the king of all beasts, yet he lacked courage. As a matter of fact, he was a coward scarred of his own shadow. On the outside, he appeared to be a normal lion. He had all the physical attributes that would lead one to believe he was the king of beasts. He had the stocky build, the razor-sharp teeth, a furry, thick coat and long, sharp, dangerous claws. He even possessed the ability to roar like a lion, a roar that would imply, "I am the king of the jungle"! As impressive as his physical appearance was and as intimidating as his roar could be, Lion was still a coward. He had all of the attributes of a lion *except* courage. Without courage, his other impressive attributes were useless and ineffective.

The only way Lion could get courage was to face his fears and experience the process of defeating the fear in his heart. All throughout his life, he had habitually shied away from facing his fear. Each time he allowed this to happen, it became easier and easier to be a coward. Before he knew it, he was nothing but a coward. Once the habitual habit of cowardice activity had rendered him ineffective, he began to search for remedies outside of himself that would "make" him courageous. In the end, he realized that courage isn't found from someone or something else, and it isn't found outside. Courage can only be given to you by you and it is found within, not without.

We are no different. Just like Lion, we become what we practice. Each time we refuse to face a fear, a portion of courage is relinquished. If we habitually shy away from fear by refusing to take it on, we develop cowardice attributes and our "courage muscle" experiences atrophy. Just like the Lion, each time we practice this behavior it becomes easier and easier to become a coward. The process of developing courage requires the opposite. It must become common practice for you to face the things that produce fear in your life. Each time you do this, you will build on the courage reserve that lies within you. Through this practice, even the most cowardly person in the world could become a model of courage.

Whether to a lion or to a human, courage has nothing to do with physical attributes. It has nothing to do with outward appearance, ethnicity, height, weight, financial standing, occupation, or any other "outside" physical thing. It has everything to do with what is on the inside.

Courage is not an attribute reserved only for the soldier going into battle, a fighter going into the ring, a firefighter risking life and limb by rushing into a raging fire to save a life or preserve another's property, or a police officer racing into the line of fire to protect an individual, family or community. Courage is available to all. It is available to the young person who chooses not to cave to peer pressure by experimenting with drugs or alcohol as his or her friends encourage them to "fit in." Courage is walking away from a confrontation as opposed to "mixing it up" with a "want to be" prize fighter. Courage is choosing not to close the business deal that will help you but hurt your client.

To be successful at anything, we must possess the courage to be something more than average. The average person in the world pops the pill, drinks the drink, takes the swing, and closes the unfair deal. The average person does whatever it takes to conform to the expectations of the world, which, I might add, isn't very much and appears to be getting less and less as the years pass.

You, however, are not average, as exhibited by your desire to read this book. This book will not appeal to the average person because the average person has no desire to learn, grow, or be challenged. The average person would rather expend effort on anything other than reading. To be something more than average is difficult and requires effort. Courage is necessary in order to become something more than average.

> *"Be strong and courageous, do not be afraid or tremble at them, for the Lord your God is the one who goes with you. He will not fail you or forsake you." Deuteronomy 31:6*

Be assured of this. You were not created to be afraid. As President John F. Kennedy once said, "*We have nothing to fear but fear itself.*" Of course, he was talking to each citizen of the United States, encouraging them to be fearless when it came to living life because he realized that the only detriment to the future of a country is a lack of action as the result of fear.

You were not born average; instead, you were born a miracle! The author of Psalm best describes you in chapter 139 verse 14. It says, "I praise you, for I am fearfully and wonderfully made. Wonderful are Your works: my soul knows it very well". You are indeed a masterpiece designed to be much more than average. You were designed for excellence. Each part of you was intricately designed with a specific purpose in mind, a spectacular purpose well beyond the realm of average.

Each precious gift of life is a miracle in itself, with endless possibilities far exceeding the standard of being average. You are much too important to choose the road of mediocrity; therefore, be of strong courage in order to become something more than average, thus leaving the world a better place simply by choosing to be something more than average. ***Before you can do something, you must be something.*** I have the Courage to be something more than average……do you?

I am Disciplined to finish what I start

Discipline is nothing more than doing what you should do when you know you should do it. Admittedly, this is easier said than done. Speaking from experience, it is much easier to crash in the recliner and take in a television program after a busy day than it is to hit the gym, even though you know the results of a trip to the gym would be much healthier and certainly more fulfilling. In this case, as in most, "easier" is not always better and so it is with discipline. Discipline to do what you should do when you should do it isn't easy, but when put into practice, it brings about tremendous results.

The practice of discipline is not always pleasant, but it is absolutely necessary for anyone desiring to find success in any endeavor in life. Discipline is perhaps one of the most difficult traits to master, but once mastered, results will follow because discipline is the attribute that puts actions to thought. It is one thing to develop a great thought but another to act on the thought. The road to failure is paved with good thoughts not acted upon. Discipline is difficult but necessary for your success. The fact that it is not easy is a good indication that it is an important attribute to possess since nearly all fulfilling things are difficult to acquire.

The world-class athlete spends years of disciplined practice to perfect their skill. The polished professional business person has found success through being disciplined to perform the activities required to find success. A straight "A" student has developed disciplined study habits required to make the grade. It is one thing to have a desire, yet another to gain possession of the thing desired through hard work and discipline. Being an amateur guitarist and drummer, I am amazed at how good a professional musician is. While playing instruments comes easier for some than others, I know of no individual who has mastered an instrument without the discipline of practice. In my estimation, Neil Peart, drummer for the rock band Rush, was one of the greatest drummers of all time. His ability to be extremely "busy" on a drum kit while maintaining precise timing was amazing. He was truly amazing for many years but was disciplined to continuously perfect his abilities. He was never satisfied with his level of ability, which again, in my estimation, was, if not the greatest ever, certainly in the top 5, and was always looking for something that would make him better. He could have easily performed flawlessly in the "drumming world" with little or no practice, but he was driven to be better. He was disciplined to improve his skills.

Whether it is playing a musical instrument, being a parent, being a spouse, being an employee or _____ (fill in the blank), to be your best requires discipline to perfect your skill. The people who rise to the top of whatever it is that they do are disciplined to invest the time required and put the work in to master the skills required to be the best.

> *"Discipline is the soul of an army. It makes small numbers formidable, procures success for the weak and esteem for all."*
> *George Washington*

Words of wisdom shared by the first President of the United States of America. As this quote by George Washington indicates, discipline is a necessary ingredient for a massive army, a small group or an army of one. Without discipline, failure is likely.

George Washington knew a thing or two about discipline as he led a rag-tag Colonial army against the mighty forces of the British Empire, which was the most powerful military force on the planet at that time. Against all odds, and there were many, the Colonial forces prevailed and birthed a country named the United States of America.

The discipline that George Washington possessed and masterfully put to use is no different than the discipline required for today's military forces around the world. It is no different from that used by successful athletic teams, successful business organizations, a successful family and yes, successful individuals like you and I. It is an absolute requirement for consistent positive results.

> *"He who ignores discipline comes to poverty and shame, but whoever heeds correction is honored." Proverbs 13:18*

Discipline sometimes requires you and I to do things that we do not always want to do. As a matter of fact, some of the things that discipline requires are absolutely unpleasant. Take, for example, your health. The formula for maintaining good health is proper diet and exercise. A bland chicken breast served with a side salad is not nearly as tasty as a juicy hamburger with fries, but it is much healthier. A rigorous exercise program is not nearly as enjoyable as sitting in the recliner with a bag of chips watching your favorite television program, but it is much healthier.

Just like everything else in life, discipline is a choice. When we understand that the development of discipline in our lives is critical to our success in whatever endeavor we pursue, we begin to gain traction toward what we desire. The lack of discipline allows us only to spin our wheels and get us nowhere in life, but once discipline is put into practice, we begin to gain traction and experience positive results. Once positive results begin to occur, the momentum builds, making what was once a very difficult task a walk in the park instead of a vertical climb up a steep mountain. Discipline is indeed the soul of an army as well as the soul of an individual.

As a universal rule, choices that produce value require discipline, which produces effort. In order to walk out of the grocery store with items in your shopping cart requires that you pay for the items or risk being arrested for theft. Before you leave the gas station, you must pay for the fuel that you pump into your automobile. To enjoy the rewards of hard work, one must be disciplined first to pay with effort. To perform otherwise will bring about the price of failure. Either way, there is a price to pay. In reality, as mentioned earlier, we don't pay the price; we reap the benefits of discipline.

Life is no different. There is a price to be paid for the worthwhile good things of this life. Health requires the discipline of proper diet and exercise, while the world prefers to seek out a miracle pill. Happiness requires the discipline of a clear mind, a clear conscience, and specific choices, while the world offers the clutter of a trendy, fast-paced lifestyle. Financial security requires the discipline of hard work and planning, while the world offers numerous get-rich-quick schemes. Life requires discipline, while the world encourages a mentality of entitlement that enslaves the unsuspecting participants of entitlement programs, stealing away dignity through a life of dependence rather than independence. Choose for yourself independence through the practice of discipline.

> *"It is true that when you discipline yourself to do the things you need to do, when you need to do them, the day is going to come when you can do the things you want to do when you want to do them." Zig Ziglar*

One of the things I love about Zig Ziglar's work is that it is always worded in very understandable terms. It doesn't take a rocket scientist or a person with a degree in psychiatry to understand the quote above. To be in a position to someday do the things we want to do when we want to do them requires that we exercise discipline today. The road to success and happiness is paved with the bricks of discipline.

If you want a bright future, you must be disciplined to begin preparing the way now. Just like a home built with a solid foundation is designed to weather the storm, the life lived with the foundation of discipline stands the test of time. Think about that for a moment. What would happen if a homebuilder skipped the process of pouring a solid foundation upon which a home would be built? The builder could spare no expense to build a home, but by skipping the process of preparing a solid foundation the home would eventually crumble away. The home may be one of the most beautiful homes ever built. The appearance of beauty would be a deceiving characteristic as the unsuspecting homeowner experienced the home begin to crack and crumble around them. The experience could have been avoided had the homebuilder simply started with a firm foundation rather than taking shortcuts.

There are no shortcuts to true success. The attribute of discipline cannot be overlooked. Continuous movement toward a goal cannot be possible without the attribute of discipline.

Is your home built on a solid foundation, undergirded with discipline or is it built on the slippery slope of ease and comfort, just waiting to be flattened by the first little puff of wind that blows your way? The choice is yours to lay the foundation of your life where you may and to be disciplined to finish what you start. ***Before you can do something, you must be something.*** I am Disciplined to finish what I start……are you?

I give a continuous, sustained Effort

How easy it is to start something that requires effort and how easy it is to quickly lose interest and give in to ease. A continuous, sustained effort is a must for anyone interested in accomplishing anything of significance.

Everyone knows that it requires a tremendous amount of effort as a professional athlete. While all professional athletes are blessed with special abilities, ability alone is not enough to remain a professional athlete. I think anyone could understand this. What about a parent, a spouse, a friend, or an employee? Do these things require a continuous, sustained effort? You had better believe it. It is easy to comprehend the fact that to be a professional athlete requires a continuous, sustained effort. It is also easy to overlook the difficulty of applying a continuous, sustained effort into the everyday activities of life.

> *"All hard work brings a profit but mere talk leads only to poverty." Proverbs 14:23*

How many times have you heard someone speak about a great plan slated to bring great results that started with all the energy one could muster and suddenly fizzled out and came to an immediate, abrupt stop? How many times has this happened to you?

Don't misinterpret this question. It is certainly good to dream. It is even better to dream big! Henry Ford's dream of a world filled with horseless carriages transformed the world of transportation. Alexander Graham Bell's dream of a device that would allow individuals from distances apart to communicate, transformed the world of communication. Mr. Ford's and Mr. Graham's dreams would have never come to fruition had they not applied effort at a continuous level necessary to accomplish the desired result. Without a continuous, sustained effort, their dreams would have died, and the world would have not benefited.

Perhaps one of the greatest examples of someone who exhibited a continuous, sustained effort was that of Thomas Edison in his pursuit of the light bulb. After struggling to develop a viable electric light bulb for months and months, Thomas Edison was interviewed by a young reporter who boldly asked Mr. Edison if he felt like a failure and if he thought he should just give up by now. Perplexed, Edison replied, "Young man, why would I feel like a failure? And why would I ever give up? I now know definitively over 9,000 ways that an electric light bulb will not work. Success is almost in my grasp." And shortly after that, after over 10,000 attempts, Edison invented the light bulb.

Source(s):

E=MC hammer · 1 decade ago

While Mr. Edison had 10,000 failed attempts before he could properly harness electrical current in a bulb to provide light, he was determined to make the continuous effort required to accomplish his objective. Can you imagine failing all those times yet continuing to fight on? Can you imagine overcoming the negative mumbo jumbo from those observers who never thought he would be successful? I am sure there were those who sneered at the idea of harnessing electrical power for the betterment of mankind. Certainly, there were those who were quite satisfied to light a candle or lantern to illuminate their homes. He may have even heard, "Why are you wasting your time"? Despite all of the obstacles and failures, Mr. Edison moved forward with a continuous, sustained effort toward success. As a result, we enjoy the benefits of his labor on a daily basis as we walk into a dark room and with a flick of a switch, a clap of a hand or even detection of our motion, the dark room is immediately illuminated.

> *"I am a great believer in luck, and I find that the harder I work, the more I have of it." Thomas Jefferson*

Dr. Kevin Elko is perhaps one of the greatest proponents of a continuous, sustained effort. Dr. Elko has used this concept to help produce national championships for the LSU Tigers and Alabama Crimson Tide football teams through invitation from coach Nick Saban. He has helped the US Olympic team, the Dallas Cowboys, the Pittsburgh Steelers, the Philadelphia Eagles, countless businesses and many individuals find success by being a proponent of a continuous, sustained effort. He has used this philosophy in tandem with others to produce the consistent performance required for success as an individual or organization. The work he has done has proven the effectiveness of the concept for organizations and individuals alike.

Having had the opportunity to spend a short moment of time with Dr. Elko, I can tell you that he is sincere in his beliefs and teachings. He practices what he preaches. I would encourage anyone to read one of his many books or listen to his "Monday Morning Cup of Inspiration," where he uploads a brief message of inspiration every Monday morning to the Cup Nation as he calls it. Certainly, if you ever have an opportunity to hear him speak make sure to take advantage of the opportunity.

It amazes me how he continues to operate at a high level, fueled by effort. He is always working hard to perfect his profession, himself and everyone around him. The results of his efforts are many changed lives. Thank you,

Dr. Elko, for what you do and how you do it. You have made many people, including myself, better because of your efforts.

A continuous, sustained effort is not easy. Notice that the theme thus far is something different than ease. Just so you know, the theme doesn't change, and as has been mentioned before, therefore, it must be beneficial. The theme doesn't change, but the results do. If you have hung in here this far, you are interested in results and not the type of person looking to take the easy way out. Likewise, you are willing to pay the price of continuous sustained effort, which is a requirement for the success that you seek. Anything of value requires effort and does not come easy.

So then, ask yourself a couple of questions. Are you giving a continuous, sustained effort in *all* important aspects of life? Perhaps you have identified areas of your life in which you have not been given the effort required to be successful. Are you willing to accept this as the truth and work toward improving those areas? Identify the important areas of your life (spiritual, family, physical, financial, professional, personal, intellectual, to suggest a few), develop a plan with daily measurable activities that will move you toward your plan and commit to the continuous sustained effort required to reach your objective.

As explained by a former manager and mentor, life is like the circus act of spinning plates. As a spinning plate loses momentum, it begins to "wobble" upon the stick. Left unattended, it will eventually fall to the ground and break. Each plate requires effort on our part to give it a push as it begins to wobble. That effort provides the momentum necessary to "spin" forward evenly and balances it again upon the stick. The process of moving from plate to plate requires a commitment toward continuous sustained effort. By sitting idly by and with no effort, the plates begin to fall one by one and shatter on the floor, but an application of continuous sustained effort keeps each plate balanced ever so carefully upon the stick. On occasion, quite often, it seems a plate or two begins to wobble, requiring our attention.

Which important plates in your life are wobbling? It could be a marriage or other family relationships, a friendship, finances, a job, school, physical health or perhaps your spiritual life. Chances are, some aspect of your life needs your attention. Will you make the effort to nudge them along or will you risk them falling to the floor and being destroyed? ***Before you can do something, you must be something***. Do you give a continuous, sustained effort?......I do.

I have Faith in the Lord God almighty, my creator, my sustainer

As I mentioned earlier, if you don't believe in something, you will fall for anything. That is so true. There are so many choices to make in a lifetime and a wide variety of things to choose from, from what style of hair, clothing, and shoes to wear to whether UFOs exist. Every belief is a personal and conscious decision.

One of the most important and influential choices that a person has the privilege of making is what and or where to place their beliefs. If you do not make those choices for yourself, there are plenty of people interested in making those choices for you. You can be assured that those people are not nearly as interested in your well-being as you are, so be wise and make those decisions for yourself.

We all have beliefs about a broad range of subjects, many of which we are willing to fall upon the sword for. While I am very passionate about my beliefs and very willing to share them with others, I have learned that it is best to understand that there are many who disagree with me. I have also found that I should not try passionately to convince someone to believe what I believe and that, most of all, I should respect the beliefs of others, whether I agree with them or not. When we are willing to do that, two things happen. My conviction of belief is tied to and only to the belief, not someone else. Secondly, if you wish for someone to believe what you believe, it is of no value to argue vehemently with someone who strongly disagrees.

One of the most hotly contested beliefs is a belief in God. I have chosen to place my beliefs and faith in the Lord God Almighty, my creator, my sustainer and my Savior. I know that there are many who do not share that belief and I will be the first to say I respect those who do not share that same belief. There is a misconception in our society that believers do not respect nonbelievers. Certainly, there are factions of believers who are not very understanding of those who do not believe as they do. While I do not understand how anyone could see and experience the many miracles of life and not believe they are a precious creation by an almighty being, I respect that decision. To the nonbeliever who may be reading this, understand that God's word is very clear about the fact that His love and our (a believer's) love is not limited to the circle of believers. We are instructed to love all people. Perhaps you have felt mistreated or misunderstood by a believer. If that is the case, I would encourage you to read what the Bible says. Not only does it have a lot to say about love, but it also has a lot to say about Grace. It is a story about the imperfection of humanity, both believers and nonbelievers and the pursuit of God, our creator, to have His creation (the human race) connect with Him. That is an extremely limited and frail attempt to explain the Bible, so I would encourage you to pick up a copy for yourself and make your own conclusion.

My belief is that there is a God who created me and created you, who loves me and loves you and has a desire to see us prosper as we love one another. I am 100% confident of that belief. I cannot imagine anyone standing before the awe of the beauty of creation, such as Tracy Arm Glacier in Alaska, the beautiful vast open plains of the Midwest United States, the tropical paradise of Hawaii, the lush green pastures of Ireland, the awesome view of Mt. Vesuvius from Pompeii or a sunrise on the Mediterranean Sea just to name a few, and not believe there is a God who created it. I see God in all of His creation's beauty and awe; I am so grateful to be a part of His most prized creation, the human race. You and I are His most prized creation. That is so hard to fathom!

There are those who do not believe that God even exists. If you are not a believer, ask yourself this one question. What if there is a God and I have spent a lifetime collecting things that will not last, impressing people who will not last and focusing on pleasure, which is here today and gone tomorrow, forever, rather than having faith in the God who created you and equipped you to live this thing we call life. As for myself, I am much encouraged to place my trust in a living God whom I will spend eternity with rather than the temporary things this "earthly" life has to offer. A trust in this short life for me would be depressing. Please remember, I am not being judgmental or critical if this is not your belief. I am not qualified to be either a judge or critic.

> *"But store up for yourselves treasures in heaven, where neither moth nor rust destroys, and where thieves do not break in or steal". Matthew 6:20*

Don't misinterpret what I am saying. If a person has been blessed with a large amount of worldly possessions it doesn't mean that they are doomed to eternal damnation. On the contrary. I believe that God enjoys seeing His people prosper financially, but He also knows that the things of this world are temporary and when we place our faith in the things of this world, disappointment and regret are sure to follow. Being a spiritual being (eternal) rather than a physical being (temporary), fulfillment for me comes from my faith in a living and loving God. Faith is the cornerstone of the believer.

> *"And he said to them, "because of the littleness of your faith; for truly I say to you, if you have faith as a mustard seed you shall say to this mountain, move from here to there and nothing shall be impossible to you.""* **Matthew 17:20**

If you desire to be a mountain mover, work hard to strengthen your faith. Faith is strengthened through trial and tribulation, so when those times come along, they will accept them as an opportunity to grow and learn rather than an obstacle. This is certainly easier said than done, but it is doable. If you can master this concept, you are ahead of the pack, but it can be mastered as anything else through repetition and practice.

So, what exactly is faith? I have heard many definitions of faith, but I believe the best definition I have ever heard came from Bob Proctor as it was passed down to him by Clarence Smithison. Bob Proctor shares the definition in his program *You were Born Rich*. He says, "Faith is the ability to see the invisible, believe the incredible and therefore receive what the world perceives as impossible."[4] Take a moment to understand the 3 components of faith as described in this definition.

The ability to see the impossible gives us the understanding that true faith is not dependent on the senses. Certainly, if you can see, smell, hear, touch, or taste something, it is almost certain to exist and, therefore, certainly believable. To see an apple sitting on the kitchen table or to taste the sweetness of the fruit validates the fact that it indeed is and apple and requires no faith to confirm this conclusion. It requires no faith to believe that the apple exists because we can see it and taste it. Therefore, it isn't hard to conclude that belief based on the senses is no faith at all. Anyone is capable of determining the existence of something seen, tasted, touched, smelled or heard. True faith is a belief based on something that cannot be accounted for by any one of the 5 senses. Faith in a living God is a personal

---

[4] Procter, Bob, 2002, "You were Born Rich", Life success productions

experience that is similar yet unlike any other person's experience as it is a personal experience, unique to each individual.

The next part of the definition is to believe the incredible. There are so many incredible things in this world. One of those things is you, me and every other human being. The intricate detail used to knit together the human body is incredible, details so small that a high-powered microscope is required to get a glimpse of what is really going on on top of and beneath the skin. As amazing as modern medicine and knowledge of human anatomy is, there is so much more to discover and learn. One could say that mankind has only scratched the surface of the exploration of human anatomy and the other amazing things in the universe, a never-ending universe that didn't just happen. It was created!

Each generation exponentially exceeds human capabilities, which would fall in the category of incredible. There was a time when there was no credibility in the belief that an individual could fly, but on an otherwise normal day, the Wright brothers made the first historic flight at Kittyhawk, NC, which changed the concept of flight from incredible to credible. Human flight is as normal as walking in this day and time. Many other incredible things are yet to be discovered and made credible to the human race. Faith is the ability to see the invisible, believe in the incredible and receive what the world believes is impossible.

There is an old church hymn that says, "nothing is impossible when we place our trust in Him", Him being God. Man can take all the credit in the world for turning the impossible into reality, but God is the creator of the universe that has such precise laws that when applied, will allow man to figure out a way to land a manned space vehicle on the moon within the fraction of a second calculated. Nothing indeed is impossible for you as you place your trust in the God who created you and this marvelous universe of which we are a tiny part.

In a lifetime, your faith will be challenged as the senses provide evidence that seems to contradict your belief. For instance, you will **hear** words of criticism and know deep in your heart that this criticism is unmerited. You will **see** others live a lifestyle that is contrary to your beliefs. Something that **tastes** good, **feels** good or **smells** good may be detrimental to your health or well-being.

When these challenges come your way, meet them head-on with faith. Know in your heart of hearts, as the Greeks described it, what is right and what is wrong. When it is all said and done, right always trumps wrong! Know who you are and what you are. Make your mind up *in advance* to respond through faith, based on values and character of who you are and what you are, to any challenges that come your way. At the time, it may not look, smell, taste, sound or feel good, but this type of intentional living will serve you well as you remain true to yourself.

If you don't believe in something, you will fall for anything. ***Before you can do something, you must be something***. I have faith in the Lord God almighty, my sustainer and my redeemer……do you?

I understand that Good is the enemy of Great

This may sound like a rather uncomfortable statement for you to grasp. We have heard all of our lives, "Just be good, or do good and everything will work out well," so why in the world would anyone not be satisfied with good? The reason is this: you, just like everything in creation, were created to flourish. You were not created to be "good enough"; you were created to be great! Does that mean that you will excel at everything that you are involved in? Of course not, but there is greatness in all of us being held hostage by the complacency of good. It also doesn't mean that you should put so much pressure on yourself to perform that there is no fun to life. The main point here is not to settle for the mediocre "you" just to get by. Light up the world by being the best "**YOU**" possible. You and the rest of the world deserve to experience your greatness.

So, how do we unleash the greatness inside? Once you have identified the things you enjoy that fit well with your talents and abilities and apply the continuous, sustained effort that we just discussed, you cannot help but be great. Understand this. Your greatness is not measured by the standard of someone else abilities. Greatness happens when you do your very best with the talents and abilities that you have been blessed with. Everyone cannot be the smartest, the fastest or the strongest, so greatness is measured by the level of achievement you reach based on your abilities.

Be careful not to use the world's standard for greatness lest you set yourself up for disaster. The world's standard of measurement for success is fame and fortune, so understand that being great does not necessarily relate to being rich and famous. Mother Theresa died with very little to no worldly possessions but was rich in the spirit of service to others. People who aspire to true greatness are not interested in riches or fame alone. Their being great at something may bring great riches and fame but true winners are interested in being the best at whatever it is that they were created to do and serving others with the talents and gifts that they have been blessed with.

I am convinced that our creator created everyone and everything to flourish, become great and do great things. I am also convinced that the creator receives glory through the flourishing of his creation. You cannot tell me that he is not happy when he sees his children perform at a high level and accomplish greatness at the level of their abilities. He has to be pleased when he sees one of his creations put to good use a talent or ability that he has blessed them with. His measure of greatness is as described, depending on the level of ability, not based on the "eyes" of the world, so something that may be minuscule to one is a great accomplishment to another. Nature abounds!

One could argue that all things do not flourish, which is accurate; however, most of nature's creation tends to flourish in a normal, healthy environment. Take Kudzu as an example. Kudzu is a vine plant native to China that was introduced to the United States to prevent soil erosion on highway right of ways. Left unchecked, Kudzu will spread well past the highway right of way, consuming anything in its path. The mighty oak tree is no match for the Kudzu plant. Over a period of time, the Kudzu plant will climb to the top of the oak tree, to the sky if necessary, eventually consuming the entire tree and choking it into submission while flourishing and seeking growth in its path.

If you drive by a "patch" of Kudzu, let it be a reminder to you that you were created to flourish, created to be great. Nothing should be allowed to get in the way, including being satisfied with good.

As youngsters, we have big dreams about great things happening in our lives. Often times, as the years go by, those dreams tend to fade for one reason or another and we tend to conform to the "normal" way of life. We become quite satisfied to live out our existence just fitting in or just getting by. The problem with fitting in is that the mold we are fitting into is molded by someone else, as discussed earlier. If we are content to "fit in" we spend our days on earth doing what others want us to do at our expense and their gain. To fit in may be considered as good. The problem is good is the enemy of great.

Not everyone can be the leader of the free world, the President and CEO of a multimillion-dollar company, a world-class athlete, a literary scholar or award-winning movie star. If you are fortunate enough to find yourself in this category, don't settle for good, settle for great. If you do not find yourself in this category, less than 1% of us will. Don't settle for good; settle for great. When you do this, you are just as great as anyone who has ever set foot on earth. Success is not measured by material possessions, job titles, physical attributes or awards. Success is measured by what you accomplish in accordance with the abilities you have.

Choose (there is that word again) to be great at whatever it is that you do. By all means, make it a priority to be a great parent, grandparent, child, grandchild, spouse, friend, worker, coworker, neighbor, citizen, employee or employer. Be a great human being. It is what you were placed here for. Always remember, "good is the enemy of great", so don't settle for anything less than great!

Imagine a world where everyone lived with the mindset of being the best they could be. It may be an unrealistic thought, but let such thought inspire you to do the only thing that you can do: your best. You are a child of God, a unique creation with talents and abilities that are unique to you. The blend of talents and abilities that make up your "recipe" is like no other. You are a perfect design with a perfect purpose. God doesn't make junk, so get about the business of flourishing. The world needs you! ***Before you can do something, you must be something***. I understand that Good is the enemy of Great. Do you?

I have created Healthy and meaningful Habits

One very interesting thing that I remember about growing up on a cattle farm was the trails created by the cattle as they made their way from one location to another. It was so interesting how they traveled the same route so often that trails, most often measuring about a foot wide, were worn into the ground. Every pasture and every wood lot was littered with "cow trails," as we called them.

While most of them led to and from a feedlot or water source, a few led to and from other locations for no apparent reason. It is as if they have their own "highway" system, much like our highway system, as favorite routes from point A to point B.

However, unlike our highway system, which is designed for each vehicle to stay in its lane, the cattle choose to stay in the same lane despite the wide-open terrain with a gazillion options from point A to point B. Day after day, year after year, generation after generation, they continue to trod the same path.

As an outdoorsman, I have noticed that many wild animals do the same thing. Most deer and other large game hunters use trails as a means to determine travel patterns of the animals in order to improve their chances of a successful hunt. Many hunters position a game camera on a noticeable trail to catch a glimpse of the animals that travel the trail. Day after day, year after year, generation after generation, these animals continue to trod the same path.

Interestingly enough, we humans are no different. We rise every morning with the same routine or ritual to begin our day; we do the same thing, go to the same places during the day, and usually finish the day with the same routine or rituals as the day before, the day before, and the day before.

There is a franchise restaurant in my hometown that is frequented daily for breakfast by retired people in the county. While there are 3 other restaurants from the same franchise within a six-mile radius, this particular location has been chosen as the preferred hangout. There are those who will drive past one of the other locations to come to this particular location for breakfast. The food is the same, the service is the same and even the building is the same, but out of habit, this location is the preferred location.

On occasion, I have stopped by to grab a quick breakfast with my daughter after an orthodontist's appointment or medical appointment not far from this location. She is always amazed at how "packed" it is when we stop. As the old saying goes, "It is so packed you can't stir them with a stick."

I am not being critical of the retired people from our part of the world for habitually frequenting the same restaurant; I am simply using it as an example of how we live our lives out of habit. They paid their dues and have earned the right to enjoy a breakfast with friends anywhere and anytime they want to. Hopefully, I will have the luxury of joining them one day.

The point you need to understand and be aware of is that we are creatures of habit and if we are not careful, it is easy to fall into unhealthy and unproductive habits. It is always beneficial to take an inventory of our habits, evaluate each one, keep the good habits and discard the ones that are unhealthy and unproductive.

Sometimes, we have habits that we know we should get rid of, but we hang on to them for one reason or another. We tend to justify our habits using a series of excuses as to why it is ok to hang on to them. Here are a few of the reasons we tend to use to justify our habits.

My parent or parents do/did it, so I can't help it because it is just in my DNA.

Nice try. While it is oftentimes true that "The apple doesn't fall far from the tree" in regards to children mimicking the behavior of parents, it is nothing more than an excuse to make bad choices and practice bad behavior just because your parent or parents did. Furthermore, there are countless examples of people who had a terrible childhood and were great achievers. Unfortunately, there are many examples of people who made bad decisions based on the influence of a parent.

I am fully convinced that there are those on one side of my own family whose lives were dramatically influenced as a result of the lifestyle that my Grandfather had. I often wondered why we spent more time with one set of Grandparents as opposed to the other set and my answer was given many years later. My Grandfather was an alcoholic and was affectionately called "By-God Willie" for his potty mouth. I must admit that I have used him as an excuse on some occasions when my potty mouth was exercised.

As a result of the alcoholic lifestyle that my Grandfather lived, many on that side of my family experienced the tragedy that comes along with alcohol and drug abuse, including horrific life-changing accidents and death. To this day, many of my relatives deal with substance abuse on one level or another. It is almost as if it were a disease passed from one generation to the next.

Fortunately for me and my sisters, my father chose not to take that route. While he did partake as a young man, once my oldest sister was born, he decided for himself on behalf of his family that it would not be part of his home. He stuck to his decision from that point on until his death. A bad habit that has passed from one generation to the next, resulting in a vicious cycle of habitual, destructive behavior.

Not only did he make that choice, but many relatives who grew up in the same situation chose the same thing for themselves and their families. By all accounts, they all live happy and successful lives. I really admire them and am really happy for them because they had every excuse available to choose a different path. A family member's bad habits do not justify your practice of the same habit. Make your own decisions and choose your own habits, good ones.

My friends are doing it.

This is apparently a universal excuse because most young people that I know and even adults, have used this excuse. I was young once and used it myself. I can remember the rationale to this day. For some reason or another, it was ok because my friend _____ did it and I really think a lot of my friend _____ so if it is ok with him/her then it is ok.

When you find yourself justifying your behavior based on that of a friend, test your hypothesis on outlandish behavior. For example, let's say that you believe, "It is ok to drink and drive because my friend _____ does it and has never had a problem with it". What you are really saying is that any behavior that your friend _____ takes part in is ok.

While there is no excuse for drinking and driving, substitute murder for drinking and driving. My friend _____ murdered someone, so it is ok for me to do the same. There are delusional people who would justify this type behavior, but my bet is that if you are reading this, you are not one of them.

Consider this. Fact is always fact and truth is always truth. In this example, there is no justification for drinking and driving. Aside from the risks for your own life are the risks posed for the innocent motorists or pedestrians whose lives are in danger as a result of your impaired state; therefore, no matter who participates in this type of behavior, it is not justifiable for you to do so. Countless lives have been lost or dramatically negatively impacted because someone justified it because a friend or someone else they knew did it.

I saw on the internet that it was okay.

In case you have not determined this for yourself, you can find an answer to anything you are looking for on the internet. If you want to substantiate your belief that plastic straws are detrimental to the environment, you can find it. If you want to substantiate your belief that the Holocaust never existed despite corroborated first-hand experience and evidence, you can find it. Whatever you are looking for, you can find it on the internet.

Newsflash: not all information found on the internet is accurate. I know that breaks the hearts of many, but it is true.

The bottom line is that just because you found evidence on the internet to justify poor behavior does not mean it is ok. Be careful what you find these days. Have an open mind. Better yet, develop good common sense.

I believe God is ok with it because the Bible says _____

Just like the internet, the Bible can be used to justify bad behavior and you better believe it is used. While I believe that the Bible is indeed the inspired word of God, I also know that it is interpreted in different ways by different people to oftentimes tell different people what they want to believe.

Just because David, whom God describes as "a man after my own heart," committed adultery with Bathsheba and had her husband sent to the front lines in battle where he was certain to die does not justify adultery or murder. One of my favorite verses is **Jeremiah 29:11**, which says, "For I know the plans I have for you says the Lord. Plans to prosper you and not to harm you, plans to give you a hope and a future". While I love this promise from the God of the Universe, I also understand that just because God has promised to prosper me doesn't mean that I can justify lazing around, doing absolutely nothing and expecting God to provide my every need.

Read the Bible. Study it from cover to cover and soak in the life-changing principles, the individual stories of success and failure, and the many promises made by an almighty God. Do these things, but by all means, do not twist the words to justify something that you know deep in your heart is not right. God gave us all a measure of common sense. Use it.

As you can see, there are a multitude of excuses we can use to justify the practice of bad habits. We didn't scratch the surface with the few that were mentioned above but hopefully, this exercise will help you evaluate your own life and identify any excuses that you might use to justify unproductive and unhealthy habits. Ultimately, there are no excuses to justify such behavior.

Use your intuition to guide you in creating good habits for yourselves. Most of us know deep down in our heart what is right for our lives and we also know that it isn't always the thing that feels good, smells good or tastes good that is best for us.

For example, I love bacon. I could literally eat 3 meals a day where bacon was the primary or even only ingredient. Whether it is a bacon-wrapped filet mignon, bacon-wrapped chicken tender, a couple of bacon slices in a pot of green beans or just plain old bacon, it is good. Bacon absolutely makes everything better; however, I know that regular consumption of bacon is not healthy, so I choose to include bacon sparingly in my diet. I do not habitually consume bacon, not because I do not like it but because I know it is not healthy and, therefore, does not fit my desire to practice healthy habits. Feel free to apply the bacon analogy to any habit that does not produce positive results. Narrow down the "bacon" habits in your life and choose to cut back on the bacon.

There is an old saying, "If it tastes good, it is probably unhealthy." While this is not an absolute truth, there is a lot of truth to it. Fatty foods, red meat, sugar, cheese, peperoni, etc., are all things that I consider to taste good, yet I limit my consumption of them all because research has shown that these foods are not healthy when consumed on a regular basis.

When we really evaluate our daily activities, I am sure we can all identify "bacon" habits that we have allowed to creep into our daily lives. They may include things like;

Excessive television watching

Excessive cell phone usage

Excessive gaming

Excessive eating

Poor diet (nighttime snacks, sweets, fatty foods etc.)

Excessive recreation

Workaholic behavior

There are many more we could add to the list, but I think you get the picture. This poor habitual activity quietly sneaks into our lives disguised as harmless activities that "everyone else is doing." There is nothing wrong with watching television. Of course not. There is also nothing wrong with using cell phones, gaming, eating (I would highly recommend you do this), snacks, sweets, fatty foods, recreation or work. All of these activities are good as long as our lives are balanced with other productive activities.

Hopefully, you realize by now that we are creatures of habit. While we have spent a lot of time discussing poor habits, we need to make it clear that all habits are not bad. Just like there is a front, there is a back; just like there is an up, there is a down; just like there is a bad, there is a good. There are good habits, just like there are bad habits.

Since we have determined that we all live our lives through a series of habits, we can determine that *in order to live a productive and meaningful life, it is very important that we create for ourselves good, productive and meaningful habits.* We must be balanced. We must intentionally determine our daily habits in alignment with the person we want to be and the things we want to accomplish.

Instead of piling up in the recliner after a long day's work or school having our brains sucked by the television for hours on end, set aside a period of time for reading, listening to motivational recordings, exercising and spending time communicating to those we love. Instead of a bag of salty, greasy potato chips as a snack, grab a juicy apple. Whatever it is that you do, make sure it is thought out and doesn't just happen.

I have found that I am happier, much more productive, and more pleasant, and I feel much better when I plan the routine for my day. I am at my best when my day is planned and performed intentionally rather than haphazardly muddling through the day, taking whatever comes, fighting fires, and accomplishing nothing.

For instance, after a cup of coffee, I like to start my day with a walk outside. During the walk, I have a prayer time, a moment of quiet before a busy day while I observe the beauty of a magnificent creation. To hear the sounds of wildlife, the breeze as it rustles through the trees, to see the magnificent colors across the landscape and to be aware of the air that flows into and out of my body. I am in my element. I am grateful for experiencing such a great life in a great place. A good start to the day usually sets the tone for the entire day.

To fulfill my desire for continuous personal growth, my day includes studying a quote and a scripture that will be memorized by the end of the week. To promote mental and physical health, at least 30 minutes should be spent in the morning, during lunch, or in the evening of exercise while listening to inspirational audio. To promote my family life, I set aside a period of undistracted time to spend with my wife and children, whether during a meal, a walk, or just quiet time.

When I am at my best, I am laser-focused on these repetitive activities and others that promote spiritual, mental, physical, and relational health. When I am at my worst, I have no focus, direction, or daily plan of action. When that happens, the tone of my day is set by others or by the circumstances that occur. This is no way to live.

Have you determined for yourself habits that produce good results? Do you live on your own predetermined terms based on your own predetermined daily habits or do you allow other people or circumstances to control your behavior, thus controlling your life?

You are the captain of your ship. You are responsible for setting the course of that ship. Programming good habits into the control system of that ship will allow you to weather the storms that are sure to come and provide safe passage into the port of your choosing. **Before you can do something, you must be something**.

Have you created healthy and meaningful habits for yourself? I have.

Integrity is important to me

In the ancient Roman empire, statues of various gods were situated in homes and businesses throughout the empire's territory. The statues were in high demand and considered to be a status symbol. Prominent people were certain to have many of them staged for the world to notice.

As a result of strong demand, it became difficult for sculptors to supply genuine, unblemished, quality statues. If the sculptor made the slightest mistake, a chunk of the statue would fall away, thus ruining the figurine. The market square was filled with various vendors who provided statues, many of which were flawed because the sculptor had experienced such a thing.

Since the demand was so high and the supply impossible to keep up with, if a flawed statue was discarded and the sculptor had to start all over again, it would be impossible to keep up with demand. To solve this problem, sculptors came up with a clever solution. If, in the process of sculpting a statue, the sculptor made a mistake that damaged the statue, rather than discard the flawed product, the wax would be applied to cover up the flaw. The process of "covering up" the flaw was so effective that detection with the naked eye was very difficult.

As this practice became more and more prevalent, there became a need to distinguish between vendors who offered "cheap" flawed statues and vendors who offered the real thing. Vendors who offered genuine statues with no defects or flaws began to display signs with the words "**sine cera**," which meant no wax. Shoppers who were looking for the real thing would look for the sine cera sign to guarantee a quality statue was being purchased. As a result, the word *sincere* was derived from sine cera to describe authenticity.[5]

If we are not careful, we live a life of insincerity. We are so wrapped up in what we want others to think and believe about us that we put on a front to disguise who we really are. We intentionally cover our flaws with wax so that we look like the genuine person we portray to the world, yet we are still flawed to the core.

If we are honest, there is a certain amount of this behavior in all of us. We all want to be liked by others. We all have a desire to "fit in" with our peeps, but if we are not careful, this desire can get out of hand and we find ourselves living a lie.

What if your life were opened for all to see? Would you be proud of what they would see? I am certain that we have all had things, whether actions or thoughts, that we would prefer to keep to ourselves but most of the time, others can see through the smoke and mirrors. Ultimately, our lives are exposed by our actions, and our integrity is put to the test, determining if our actions align with who we portray ourselves to be.

Living a life of integrity doesn't just happen; it happens because it is made a priority in our lives. For it to become a priority, we must become aware of our every thought and action and apply the integrity test;

Is this in alignment with who I portray myself to be?

Is this something that I would be proud of for others to know about?

Does this positively affect others?

5 Waitley, Denis, 1983, "Seeds of Greatness" Simon and Schuster

Would I want my child to do this?

If the answer to any of these questions is "no, " then we should stay away from it.

Living with integrity is not something that is always easy. As a matter of fact, it is difficult. We live in a world full of distractions, all of which will throw us off of our game. We all have thoughts, desires, and traits that must be kept under control.

I will reluctantly expose myself to the world concerning a trait that I must control. My Grandfather's nickname was "By-God Willie" because of the colorful language that he chose to use. I am sorry to say that his Grandson (me) has to really be careful or that same colorful language will flow effortlessly from my mouth.

I would prefer for the world to believe that I am one who always speaks eloquently and doesn't use poor language. I am even aware that cursing is a sign of ignorance, yet I occasionally find myself ignorant. I find myself being someone whom I do not portray to the world as being. I find myself with little integrity.

While it is difficult to be transparent about such a shameful flaw, I am willing to share it with the world in the hopes of illustrating the importance of integrity. I will also declare that this character flaw nor any other will keep me from pursuing a life of integrity, which I consider a tremendous attribute to aspire toward.

I am certainly ashamed of my lack of integrity and aware of its influence on me and those around me. As a result of my awareness, I realize the importance of striving to be an individual of integrity. When I intentionally live the life that aligns with who I say I am, my life and the lives of those around me are more pleasant.

> *"The integrity of the upright guides them, but the unfaithful are destroyed by their duplicity." Proverbs 11:3*

> *"A good name is more desirable than great riches; to be esteemed is better than silver or gold." Proverbs 22:1*

Your name is important. Not necessarily how it is spelled or pronounced but what your name says to others about who you are. What is important is what others know you to be when they hear your name.

I could name a person or two who everyone knows is unpleasant to be around for one reason or another. They have chosen for themselves to have an abrasive personality made up of hateful speech and action. It is as if they are miserable; therefore, they want you to be miserable. They have no regard for how their speech or actions affect others. They selfishly spew reckless speech from their mouths and engage in activities with no regard for others. They have zero integrity.

On the other hand, I could name those people I know to be encouraging, kind, loving and respectful to others. We are attracted to these people because we know they care about us and have our best interests in mind.

We should all aspire to be an individual whose speech and actions are uplifting to others. Others should know that we are genuinely loyal, honest, caring, and loving. Our speech is uplifting and encouraging. Our word is genuine and true. Our handshake means something other than an act; it is a gesture of honor. Our actions promote the betterment of those around us.

When we live with integrity, we can look confidently into someone's eyes and speak the truth, knowing we will deliver on the words we speak. We can be brutally honest with ourselves and others about who we are. We are who we say we are. Our name has meaning.

> *"What lies behind us and what lies before us are tiny matters compared to what lies within us." Ralph Waldo Emerson*

Integrity is something that is deep inside of us, protected from the ways of the world and those who have nothing better than to ruin our name. It is not influenced by our environment.

Chameleons are interesting little creatures. In order to protect themselves from predators, they are able to change the color of their skin to blend perfectly with their environment. I have observed them quite often around our home. If they are perched on a green plant, the color of their skin changes to the green color of the plant. If they are stationed upon the brick of our home, the color of their skin is the color of the brick. If they move from one to the other, their skin color changes before your eyes. They change their appearance to match their environment.

If we are not careful, we live our lives in the same manner as the Chameleon. We change who we are to reflect the environment we find ourselves in. In an attempt to "fit in," when we are in with the party crowd, we party. When we are in a crowd of people using foul language, we develop a potty mouth. When we are around "church folks", we act like church folks. We adapt to our environment to "fit in" and appease others. We become whomever we need to become to be part of the crowd.

Are you a Chameleon? Does your behavior change to adapt to the environment you are in? Do you live a life of integrity or do you just go with the flow and "fit in"?

For some reason, we sometimes believe that others will respect us more by adapting our behavior to match their behavior even though it is not who we really are. We believe that others will like us if we go along with the crowd. In reality, others respect individuals who are who they say they are. They respect individuals with integrity and most importantly, individuals with integrity respect themselves.

Have respect for yourself. Be who you say you are. If you are a green lizard, be a green lizard. If you are a red lizard, be a red lizard. It is not what is on the outside that matters; it is what is on the inside. It is your integrity. Be proud of who you are. Live up to your expectations, not the expectations of others.

Are you a person with integrity? Are you a "what you see is what you get" person? Can you be trusted to be who you say you are? These are great questions to ask yourself. Practice daily to live a life of integrity so you can answer with a resounding "YES."

Before you can do something, you must be something. Are you a person of integrity? I am.

I am not subject to the Judgment of others

The number one barrier to a happy and prosperous life is fear. The number one fear is the fear of what others would think. In some cases, that is not a bad thing. For instance, you should be concerned about what others think as it relates to the laws of the land or moral issues. If you hold up a bank or maliciously injure another person, you should be subject to the judgment of others. If you are dishonest with others, then you should face the consequences and accept that your name is tarnished. You should not, however, be concerned about what another person thinks about such things as the way you look, the clothes you wear, the vehicle you drive, the home you live in, or the size of your bank account.

This does not mean that we should not look our best, wear our best or be our best. We should always be, look, and act as best we can.

However, it is a waste of time and energy to give a thought to what anyone thinks about you if you were to fail at business, what type of occupation you have, what type of home you live in or what type of car you drive. If you drive your clunker car from your outdated small home to your job, which barely pays enough for you to survive, then that is your business and yours alone. I did it for many years, and I am not too good to do it again.

I can remember a time right after I graduated from college when I did not have a "professional" job. I worked on a farm for $3.00 per hour, worked a construction job laying tile, cleaned toilets, cut grass, dug holes with a pick and shovel and swept floors with a college degree.

I wasn't too good for it then and I am not too good for it now, but I must admit I was concerned about what others thought of me. I was so concerned about what others thought about me spending all those years in college and not landing a high-paying career. I had friends who chose to go to work directly out of high school, had better jobs, and made a better income than I did.

To make things worse, I had to move back in with my parents. I loved my parents, but I had lived an independent lifestyle for 5 years (I was on the 5-year plan not because of grades but because I couldn't settle on a major, so don't be judgmental). For five years, I could come and go as I pleased and here, I was living back at home with my parents.

It was not a pleasant experience, not because of the atmosphere, but because of what I believed others thought of me. I even wondered if my parents questioned their decision to send me to college.

Don't live your life wondering what others think about you. Instead, live your life free from the fear of judgement.

You are not subject to the judgment of others. Be proud of yourself as long as you are an honest, loving, law-abiding, productive human being. The world is full of dishonest, uncaring outlaws driving nice vehicles and living in a sprawling mansion. Don't get me wrong, there are many very good people who drive nice vehicles and live in a sprawling mansion, but it is not the nice vehicle or the sprawling mansion that makes the person, despite how our society often judges others by the "things" they have.

> *"What someone else thinks about me is none of my business."*
> *Eleanor Roosevelt*

What a powerful statement. We could only imagine the potential of removing the chains placed on us by *our* own thoughts of what *someone else* thinks about us. The chains of thought will prove to keep us in bondage if we allow ourselves to place value on what others think of us in regards to the petty, meaningless things of life. Our value is not determined by our looks, the vehicle we drive, the clothes we wear, the home we live in, the size of our home, or any other meaningless worldly criteria of measurement. Our value is what lies within us, not what is visually seen and perceived by others. I have made a lot of money through the years, owned many nice vehicles and lived in a nice home, but my paycheck, my vehicle and my home are not what makes me me. I literally do not care what anyone else thinks about me because I know who and what I am, period.

You are a unique creation of the almighty God, gifted with unique traits and special talents. If the God of the universe took such care to make you exclusive from the rest of his mighty creation, then who could be critical of the masterpiece "YOU"? You do not need physical possessions or someone else's approval to be special. Just be special. Be YOU!

Every star that shines in the night sky is placed there for a reason. Every grain of sand, drop of water, or any other creation, as insignificant as they may seem to be, is magnificent and was created specifically by design and for a specific purpose. If a grain of sand is a magnificent creation, then think of how special you are. You were created for this place and for this time, so do not allow another person to steal your significance by allowing their judgement to make you feel any less as a person.

You are specifically and uniquely gifted for a very important purpose. While we are not all created to be a famous leader, a great artist, a wonderful public speaker, a professional athlete or a spectacular musician, we are all created for greatness. If we were all spectacular musicians, we could not appreciate the beauty of a great musical performance. If we were all great artists, we could not appreciate a masterpiece. You *are* the masterpiece. You were created intentionally for a specific purpose.

The beauty of you is the intricate design and detail that was given by your creator to create you just the way you are. You are a masterpiece. Do not let the judgement of others extinguish the greatness that lies beneath the surface, waiting to bring positive changes to your part of the world.

You are a child of God. Your living small does not serve the world. Marianne Williamson

Yes indeed. You are a child of God. The magnificence and significance of your creation is not to be underappreciated by yourself or anyone else. Your specific purpose is important to your generation. Put those gifts to work to serve the world. In turn, you will be served as well. When you understand this, you also understand that the judgement of others is not important. It is irrelevant.

Be very careful about your own self-evaluation as well. It is productive to evaluate your strengths and weaknesses in order to maximize your strengths and minimize your weaknesses, but avoid at all cost comparing yourself to others or thinking of yourself as less important or less valuable.

We can't all be the biggest, the strongest or the smartest, nor are we designed to be. We are designed to be unique. Success is not measured by how well we do when compared to others. Remember, success is measured by how well we do compared to how well we could have done with our abilities. We are not in competition with another to see who is the greatest; we are in competition with ourselves to see how great we can be based on the abilities and gifts we have been given.

If I were to compare my "worldly" value to that of a professional athlete, the perception of my value would not be good. While I would consider myself athletic and participated in high school athletics, my athletic skill level compared to a professional athlete would not score high. If the number one basis for value was athletic ability, my value would fall short as compared to a professional athlete.

I know, however, that I am just as valuable as a human being as any professional athlete that ever lived and so are you. You are extremely valuable and do not let anyone convince you otherwise.

You will always have those who will judge you for one reason or another. You may not look like them, believe as they believe or even talk like they talk. Go ahead, accept this fact, deal with it and move on.

Just as important as it is not to allow another's judgement of us to have value, it is also important not to practice judging others. When you find yourself in the crowd passing judgement on another, find yourself in another crowd. The people I know who refuse to criticize and pass judgment on others in a group setting are the people I respect most and they are the people I really trust not to pass judgement on me in the presence of others.

For some reason or another, our human nature just loves a juicy story. If someone else does something "bad," we can easily get involved in a group discussion, passing judgement on this unfortunate soul discussing amongst ourselves how we would never stoop that low, justifying in our mind that it really isn't gossip. We are only discussing it because we are concerned about the poor soul.

I have learned to never say never. Be careful when you pass judgement on another lest you fall victim of the same vice yourself. We would all be better served to leave judgement to the courts and the Almighty God.

Have you allowed your value of yourself to be diminished by the judgement of others? Is your life controlled by what other people think about you? Have others been negatively affected by the judgement you have placed upon them? If you can answer yes to any of these questions, there is work to do.

Begin today to live your life based on the positive perception of yourself rather than the judgement of others. Understand the magnificence of you as a unique, one of a kind human being. Know deep in your heart that your value is not determined from the outside; it is determined by what is on the inside, the belief that "I am not subject to the judgement of others.

Before you can do something, you must be something. Are you subject to the judgement of others? I'm not.

I am Kind to everyone

Being kind to everyone can be very difficult, especially when the world has a plentiful supply of unkind people. It seems as though our society deems it gain to be unkind to others, whether it is taking advantage of another's weakness or "flipping off" the driver who got *your* parking place as if this type of behavior builds one's esteem by establishing dominance. On the contrary, it is a sign of weakness. The dominant person takes the high road, avoids conflict when possible and promotes kindness to others.

When we are kind to others, it not only positively affects others but also positively affects us. It feels good to be kind to others. It brings joy to be able to put a smile on someone's face with an act of kindness.

There are those who are just downright mean. I don't like being around them; you don't like being around them; no one likes being around them. They are so unkind they don't even like being around themselves.

There are those who believe being kind is a sign of weakness. They believe it is a sign of strength to be unkind.

I know of a gentleman whom we will call George to protect his privacy. George consistently treated others unkindly and even boasted how his "in-your-face personality" was important to his business. He believed that he could bully others to do business with him, and he couldn't care less about what anyone thought about him.

He was indeed successful in the eyes of the business world, racking up countless awards and accolades. His business flourished and it seemed that his unkind demeanor was indeed a successful strategy, that is, until it caught up with him. His cocky, unkind personality finally caught up with him by belittling his superior in public. The very thing that appeared to bring him success spelled his demise. Karma definitely dealt with George.

The odd thing about George is that he actually thought others respected him when, indeed, none of his peers had any respect for him. His bully mentality led him to believe he was above reproach.

I was sorry to see George lose his job, but it could be seen coming from a mile away. It was obvious that George was talented and that if he could have channeled his personality, he would have been a huge success. George's story was a perfect example to myself and others that one's unkindness toward others will eventually catch up to them.

How hard is it to be kind? How hard is it to smile when we see another person? Certainly, there are those whom we find it difficult to be kind to because of their personality, but in general, it is not difficult to be kind to others.

We have a choice to set the tone anytime we encounter another soul. Kindness is a gift that should be nurtured. It should be kept near and dear to the heart. Simply put, to serve the world with kindness is to be served.

What are you getting? Are others kind to you? If not, maybe you should take a look at your kindness meter. There are certainly those who do not have a kind bone in their body or who will respond to kindness. I could name a few and I am sure you could, too. It really must be a miserable existence to be an unkind person. When you encounter one of those miserable souls, don't wallow in their misery. Be kind and experience the joy of kindness for yourself at a minimum and who knows, you may have an opportunity to change their life forever.

Being unkind is a character flaw. It is either a selfish act of defiance or evidence of poor self-image or poor self-esteem. In the case of defiance, the person, for whatever reason, chooses to act in a manner that defies the unwritten rules of a civil society. Their mission is to be unkind to others and they are proud of it. Chances are being unkind is not the only act of defiance they are engaged in.

In the case of self-image or self-esteem issues, a person feels the need to find self-worth by mistreating others, so perhaps the other person will feel inferior, too. Whatever the case may be, don't participate as a giver or taker of unkindness. It is a very unhealthy and undesirable activity.

The most effective way to get kindness is to give kindness. It is true that in life, you most often get what you give. If you don't believe me, observe the lives of others and gather evidence for yourself. Notice how the bitter person attracts bitterness, the evil person attracts evil, and the hateful person attracts hatred. Also, notice how the helpful person attracts help, the loving person attracts love and the kind person attracts kindness. While there are countless examples of bad things happening to good people, there are exponentially more examples of others getting what they give.

We have all experienced the great feeling as a receiver of kindness, but the beauty of kindness is its impact on the giver. There is no greater feeling in the world than shining a little sunshine on someone's day, whether it be a gentle smile, a refreshing greeting or an act of kindness like holding the door for someone or assisting someone in need. Take every opportunity, and that is what it is, an opportunity to be kind to others. Daily practice of this will literally fill your heart with joy as well as others around you.

What does your Joy meter register? It is somewhere between empty and full, and only you can read the meter.

> *"A generous man will prosper; he who refreshes others will himself be refreshed." Proverbs 11:25*

Mother Theresa may have been the kindest person who ever breathed. She devoted her life to giving everything that she had to the needy. At her death, she did not have a healthy bank account, a mansion on the hill, or a yacht to sail the ocean blue. She did, however, have the respect of anyone who was anyone, which is more than can be said for countless individuals with healthy bank accounts, a mansion on the hill or a yacht to sail the ocean blue.

Her life of serving others has blessed not only those that she served but also anyone who simply observed her unselfish service. Without a doubt, her life of kindness and service not only touched the people she served and was a perfect blueprint to the world of the impact kindness to our fellow man or woman can have. Her Joy meter had to be passed full!

What about you? Are you kind to others? Will you be remembered fondly as someone who genuinely cared about others and expressed that genuine care through acts of kindness or will you be the one gratefully forgotten because you made it your objective in life to sow discord and strife by being unkind to others? What legacy are you creating?

Before you can do something, you must be something. Positively affect your life and the lives of others by being kind to those you encounter. What a great world we would live in if everyone would practice a little kindness.

I Love the Lord my God with all my heart and my neighbor as myself.

Love is the most powerful word in the world. There is nothing that can compare to being loved by others and also loving others. Both being loved by others and loving others bring great joy to the soul.

The roots of love can be traced to creation itself. The creator, God, created human beings, His most prized creation, for the purpose of loving and being loved by them. Since the Bible describes God as love, then it would stand to reason that His most prized creation, human beings, created in His own image, would have the need to love and be loved. Love, therefore, did not evolve; it was present from the very beginning.

If you want to live a happy and productive life, you must love others. The purest measure of love is that in which we put the interest of others ahead of our own. When we truly love others, we care about their needs and we respond to their needs accordingly. We never take advantage of their need as a means of promoting ourselves or our ambitions. When we love others, we are selfless in our service toward them, always having their best interest in mind.

Loving others, however, does not always mean we give them what they want. For example, a child who has no respect for a parent and hardly ever follows the rules set forth by the parent and wants the freedom to come and go as they please. The loving parent will deny what the child wants and do everything in their power to do what is best for the child.

While love is the most powerful thing in the world, it may also be the most misused and misunderstood word as well. One friend tells another, "I love you," one minute, and the next minute, they are bashing them in the presence of another "friend." With friends like that, who needs enemies?

First and foremost, don't be that friend. Most of us have been guilty of being disloyal at one time or another, but we understand it is never the right thing to do. This type of activity is a direct indication that you are not to be trusted nor believed. Your words will hold no meaning to those who really know you if you partake in this type of activity. Any respect that others might have had will quickly be lost, much more so than it was found.

Second of all, don't let another person, whether friend or foe, steal your joy by allowing their words to hurt you. The old saying, "Sticks and stones may break my bones, but words will never hurt me," says it all.

We have all been the subject of unkind talk, which I like to call chatter. The responsibility of chatter falls on the chatterer, not the subject of chatter, as should the consequences. As Eleanor Roosevelt so eloquently stated, "*What someone thinks of me is none of my business.*" The next time someone unwarranted speaks negatively about you, let the words go in one ear and out the other having no effect on you at all.

When we love others, we speak kindly about them and to them. It is our duty to take responsibility for the words we speak but not those spoken by others. Make sure not to be an *innocent* bystander, either. It may be tempting to hear all about the circumstances Jane Doe has found herself in but it serves no purpose to be a part of the conversation as an *interested listener.* Chances are you will find yourself in an interesting circumstance on occasion, so you could very well find yourself the subject of conversation.

When Jesus was asked which commandment was the greatest of all, He answered:

> ***Love the Lord your God with all your heart and with all your soul and with all your mind. This is the first and greatest commandment. And the second is like it; Love your neighbor as yourself. Matthew 22:36-40***

All of the evil that exists in the world could be vanquished if this were the creed of all people. The entire world would be a utopian society in which everyone would flourish and prosper in. Can you imagine it? No more wars, no more fighting, no hatred, no greed or dishonesty, among other things. I suppose if this were to happen, the lock manufacturers and installers would go out of business, but I believe they would find themselves in a better place, too. We would all be unified and looking out for the best of others. Wow! What a world it would be.

As you read this, you may be saying to yourself, "It would be good, but it will never happen, so there is no reason for me to try to change it." You may be correct that it will never happen, but you are wrong to assume that if you do nothing to make it better, then you assume no responsibility for the condition of the world.

If Helen Keller, who became deaf and blind at a very early age, had thought, "I will never see nor hear, so there is no need to try to improve my life," thousands of people who were served by her determination to improve her life despite her condition would have remained under the bondage of their condition. She did indeed never see nor hear, but it did not stop her from being the first blind and deaf person to earn a college degree and be a strong advocate for people who were deaf and blind. Her perseverance alone has inspired an untold number of people to rise above a negative condition and excel despite the negative condition.

Never sell yourself short. What you do, what you say, how you live, and how you love matters! It matters to those around you and to those around them because to share the condition of true love is such a desirable attribute and has such a profound effect on others that it is contagious. No human being with a heart can experience the power of love and not be changed for the better.

Nelson Mandela, South Africa's first democratically elected President, once said, "***Your living small does not serve the world.***" This is one of my favorite quotes, also quoted by Marianne Williamson, because it is a reminder to everyone that we are all created to serve the world in a big way. We may not all be the President of a country, a famous musician or movie star or anything other than a little-known person in our corner of the world, but that doesn't mean we cannot live a life of significance. Prior to Mandela being elected President, he spent several years behind bars as a political prisoner. Had he resigned his existence to being a prisoner, he would have never "lived largely and served the world."

Have you resigned your existence to living small, or do you understand that there are greater things for you to accomplish? Do you love the Lord God with all your heart and your neighbor as yourself? If so, keep it up. If not, get busy today loving the one who loved you first and created you to his exact specifications so you can flourish in this world and then get busy loving his other human creations. Get busy changing the world one person at a time by sharing the precious gift of love.

People who love others promote others through not only their speech but their actions. Don't just tell someone how much you love someone, show them. Actions speak louder than words. I have a feeling that my wife is going to bookmark this page and highlight that sentence for the convenience of reminding me to always do that 😊.

It is easy to tell someone that we love them, but sometimes it is difficult to show them, especially if they have said or done something to "hurt" our feelings. Chances are great that, at some time or another, that special someone is going to do or say something to "hurt your feelings." To all of you out there whom I truly love, and there are many, I am not perfect; therefore, I will let you down…….but I still love you.

Forgiveness plays such a major role in our relationships. Forgiveness is not only an act that promotes love toward an individual who has wronged us, but it also promotes psychological health to the forgiver by removing the focus from the act and placing it on the value of the other person. I might add that in order to forgive someone, you must first love and respect yourself.

Is forgiveness easy? Heck no, but it is healthy and crucial for a strong, loving relationship.

Let's face it. We are all different people, very different in many ways. As a result, it is easy to pass judgement at best or at worst, practice hatred.

> *"Hatred stirs dissension but love covers all wrong."*
> *Proverbs 10:12*

We are all created to love our creator and our neighbor as ourselves. Can you imagine a world where people lived to love others? What a wonderful world it would be. Be a world changer. Live large by loving large.

Before you can do something, you must be something. Do you love the Lord your God Almighty with all of your heart and your neighbor as yourself? I do.

I have an incredible unlimited Mind

The human mind is such an incredible thing. Similar to a computer that operates a machine, it is the CPU (Central Processing Unit) of the human machine. It controls everything from the unconscious, such as breathing, putting on clothes, and tying shoes, to the conscious, such as deciding which clothes to wear, what to eat, and which vehicle to purchase. Needless to say, the mind is extremely powerful.

Since it is so powerful, it is extremely important to keep guard of it 24/7, protecting it and us from harm. There is an old computer jargon that states, "garbage in, garbage out," which implies that poor programming (what goes in) will yield poor results from the computer (what comes out). If we squeeze Orange Juice into a cup, the cup will not yield Apple Juice as the contents are removed. And so it is with the mind that what is fed into the mind will certainly determine what experiences pour from the human life.

Raymond Holliwell, in his book "Working with the Law," gives a detailed description of the power that each of our minds possess. An understanding of this power and how to harness it is extremely important to each individual's success or failure.

Holliwell says, "Scientists tell us that thought is compared with the speed of light. They tell us that thoughts travel at the rate of 186,000 miles per second."

Our thoughts travel 930,000 times faster than the sound of our voice. No other force or power in the universe yet known is as great or as quick. It is a proven fact, scientifically, that the mind is a battery of force, the greatest of any known element. It is an unlimited force; your power to think is inexhaustible, yet there is not one in a thousand who may be fully aware of the possibilities of his thought power. We are mere babes in handling it. As we grow in understanding and in the right use of thought, we will learn to banish our ills and establish good in every form we desire. It is our power to think that determines our state of living. As one is able to think, he generates a power that travels far and near, and this power sets up a radiation that becomes individual as he determines it. Our thoughts affect our welfare and often affect others we think of. The kind of thoughts we register in our memories or habitually think, attract the same kind of conditions.

If we take the thought of success and keep it in mind, the thought elements will be attracted, for "like attracts like." We are mentally drawn to the universal thought currents of success, and these thought currents of success are existent all around us. We will psychically contact minds who think along the same lines, and later, such minds will be brought into our lives.

Therefore, successful-minded people help success come to them. That is how successful living is founded. The Law of mind is in perpetual operation and works both ways. Persons who dwell on thoughts of failure or poverty will gravitate toward like conditions; they, in turn, will draw to them people who accept failure and poverty. On the other hand, we can think of positive conditions, on success and plenty, and in the same manner, enjoy full and plenty. What the mind holds within takes its form in the outer world." [6]

---

6   Holliwell, Raymond, 2008, "Working with The Law", BN Publishing

He goes on to say, "The mind force is creating continually like fertile soil. Nature does not differentiate between the seed of a weed and that of a flower. She produces both seeds to grow. The same energy is used for both, and so it is with the mind. The mind creates either good or bad. Your ideas determine which is to be created".

Bob Proctor in his magnificent book, "You were born rich" explains the magnificent power of the mind. He says, "Dr. Alexander Rich, Professor of Biophysics at M.I.T., has estimated our central nervous system contains from 10 to 100 million cells, each one of which has a storage capacity equal to that of a large computer. If his estimates are even close to being correct, it would imply that the human mind has the capacity to store all of the known information in the world- with room to spare.

Other specialists in the field of human creativity are similarly convinced that all people have uncharted reservoirs of untapped potential locked up within the confines of their incredible minds. For example, Dr. W. Ross Addey of the Space Biology Laboratory of the Brain Research Institute at U.C.L.A. has said that, The ultimate creative capacity of your brain may be, for all practical purposes, infinite".[7]

One could easily conclude from Holliwell's and Proctor's analysis that the mind is by far the most powerful tool in the human arsenal. Physical brawn, no matter the extent of strength, is no match for the mind. To train the mind through repetitive daily right thinking, research and habitual practice will pay huge dividends to the individual who is willing to put in the work. To train the mind in proper thinking cannot be overemphasized. Discipline yourself to fuel the mind with proper thinking on a daily basis and the results will undeniably deliver great dividends.

There are many distractions in the world, some more harmful than others. It is imperative to be aware of these distractions and steer away from them, even the things we consider "small things," whether a thought or action that

---

[7] Proctor, Bob, 2002, "You were born Rich", Life Success Production

would move you "slightly" off course. Every "slight" movement off course puts you that much farther off course. Think of it like this. If you are flying from Atlanta Hartselle airport to LAX in Los Angeles, a slight one degree of variation off course, could land you in Mexico or Canada.

Everyone experiences variations off course, from time to time. We all have unwanted things in our lives as a result of our input (thoughts). A detour from time to time is to be expected, but the important thing is to recognize those times and make corrections ASAP to get back on course.

There is a stream that runs through our farm. A pipe has been installed to allow movement from one side of the stream to the other. Some years ago, heavy rains washed several dead limbs and other clutter down the stream. When the limbs reached the pipe, they became lodged in the entrance of the pipe. Soon after, other clutter, such as sticks and leaves, quickly collected around the larger limbs. Over time, the pipe was completely stopped up with the debris, causing water to flow into the fields on both sides of the stream, making it very difficult to travel across the stream and flooding the fields. Leaving the pipe stopped up would have ultimately led to the erosion of the fields, rendering them useless. The pipe in this condition no longer served its purpose and left unattended, would cause further damage.

With a little time and effort, the debris was removed from the entrance of the pipe, the water began to flow through its natural channel, the fields dried and navigation across the stream was again easy. The water once again flowed in the proper channel. Through proper attention and effort, the pipe served its purpose as the water was channeled in the right direction.

Our minds work the same way. If we are not careful, clutter from outside sources (thoughts from outside sources such as other people, television, magazines, social media etc.) accumulates over a period of time. If we are not careful to remove the clutter, it accumulates gradually until our "right thinking" turns to "stinking thinking." Our streams of clear thought are gradually blocked, producing poor results. If not corrected a vicious cycle of poor thoughts leading to poor results spirals out of control.

The mind is no different than a muscle in the body. When left idle, it develops atrophy; when exercised, it flourishes and grows; therefore, it is very important to exercise the mind with the good, the pure, and the positive. Be proactive by studying, reading and observing things that will produce knowledge and wisdom which is something that can never be taken from us. Once we have it, it is ours forever.

> *"Learning is the beginning of wealth. Learning is the beginning of health. Learning is the beginning of spirituality. Searching and learning is where the miracle process all begins." Jim Rohn*

There are so many things to learn and experience in life. Take every opportunity to expand your incredible mind, better understand how things work and develop better ways of doing things. Keep an open mind to better ways of accomplishing things and living life to the fullest. Use the most powerful tool in your possession to your benefit and the benefit of others—Your incredible, unlimited mind. **Before you can do something, you must be something.**

I have an incredible, unlimited mind. How about you?

I will Never, Never, Never quit

One of the greatest success stories of all times is the story of Abraham Lincoln. The fact that he was elected president of the United States of America, though a tremendous accomplishment, is not what makes the story so great. The story is great because of the many failures that he endured in his pursuit of success. He simply refused to quit and as a result, he was elected the 16th President of the United States. This is what preceded his election.

1831   Failed in business

1832   Defeated for Legislature

1833   Second Failure in business

1836   Suffered nervous breakdown

1838   Defeated for Speaker

1840   Defeated for Elector

1843   Defeated for Congress

1848   Defeated for Congress

1855   Defeated for US Senate

1856   Defeated for Vice President

1858   Defeated for US Senate

1860   Elected President[8]

Lincoln's challenges had just begun. As the 16th President, his "never quit" attitude and beliefs served him well as he guided a divided country through civil war and preserved the Union. One would have to believe that the many challenges he faced throughout his life and the "no-quit" attitude he had developed as a result had prepared him for such a task.

> *"And let us not grow weary of doing good, for in due season we will reap, if we do not give up." Galatians 6:9*

The ability to never quit is a special and noble attribute. It is an attribute possessed by all successful people. It is an attribute that is absolutely necessary to have and must be part of our character. It is the special attribute that made it possible for an exiled, fallen Prince to become Shepherd, Moses, to lead the Israelites out of slavery in Egypt. It is the special attribute that made the Shepherd boy David, a hero by defeating a giant despite his boyish physical attributes and a King of the ages despite his many failures and many enemies. It is the special attribute that can move you from a life of insignificance to a life of significance.

There are occasions when it is easy to throw up our hands and quit. I played on a high school athletic team, which gave me an early taste of quitters. We had a very talented individual on our team who could have contributed greatly to our success. About a week before our opening game, he and others chose to quit the team for reasons I am unaware of. I will never forget the feeling of disgust that I had. All of the work we had put in toward a successful year didn't mean anything to these people as they

---

[8]   Grossman, Ned, 1999, "How to Succeed in Life", Diamond publishing company

just turned in their gear and went about their daily lives. It had a profound effect on me. At that time, in my eyes, he would always be a quitter, but most importantly, as a result of the negative impact it had on me and my other teammates, it made me vow to never, never, never quit.

It is ingrained in my DNA not to be a quitter at anything, big or small. I intend to always finish what I start.

Of course, maturity and time passed, which allowed me to be less judgmental and more forgiving toward this person. Perhaps there were underlying reasons that I was unaware of that forced him to quit. While I would never offer an excuse for quitting, I do believe everyone deserves our grace.

Whatever the case may be, quitting is not an option for me, nor should it be for you. When you start something, finish it. When you obligate yourself to someone to do something, do it. When you take a job, do it and do it well. There is nothing wrong with bettering yourself and moving to another job, but make the move with dignity. Be grateful to your current employer and give them the customary 2-week notice that they deserve and need to properly conduct business.

Show up, do what you obligated yourself to, and do it right, whether you like it or not. Remember this: winners never quit and quitters never win. Can you tell that I am a little passionate about this one?

Win or lose, everyone appreciates someone who refuses to quit. There is just something about a person with true grit and determination to see something through that is important to them. Whether on the battlefield, on the athletic field of play, in the business world, or in everyday life, legends are born through a tenacious appetite to press forward toward a worthy goal and never quit.

Before you can do something, you must be something. I will Never, Never, Never quit. How about you?

I see only the Objective. Obstacles must give way

It was Napoleon Bonaparte who spoke these words. Like him or not, he was successful at what was important to him: conquering opposing armies. Napoleon had a vision of what he wanted to accomplish and allowed nothing to get in the way of his vision of victory. His physical stature was said to be small, but his vision was huge.

It is also important for us to develop a clear picture in our mind of what it is in life that we want to accomplish. Once we have decided specifically what we want to accomplish, it is critical to develop a clear picture of our lives once we have successfully acquired it.

Philosopher and author James Allen writes about the power of vision in his classic book "As a man Thinketh." He says, "Dream lofty dreams, and as you dream, so shall you become. Your vision is the promise of what you shall one day be; your ideal is the prophecy of what you shall at last unveil. The greatest achievement was, at first and for a time, a dream. The oak sleeps in the acorn; the bird waits in the egg. And in the highest vision of a soul, a waking angel stirs. Dreams are the seedlings of realities. Your circumstances may be uncongenial, but they shall not remain so if you only perceive an ideal and strive to reach it. You cannot travel within and stand still without".[9]

The message in this eloquent use of words may sound mystical and difficult, but to the contrary, it is, as one once said, "as right as rain". Very simply put, everything begins with a vision…..a dream. With the unlimited potential of the incredible mind that we discussed earlier, do yourself a favor and dream "lofty dreams," dream big. You were created for great things. To achieve great things, one must think great thoughts and dream big dreams. Never underestimate the power of your dreams, and never listen to the doubters that your dreams are unachievable. Your critics are most likely individuals who lack the courage and fortitude to pursue a lofty dream and most certainly enjoy having others join them in their misery of little or no accomplishment.

> *"You are a child of God. Your playing small does not serve the world." Marianne Williamson*[10]

You were created and designed for success. There is no debate that all were created for this very purpose, yet many forgo the privilege and opportunity to succeed, whether as the result of poor self-image, poor work ethic, or ignorance of the degree of potential that one possesses. Whatever the case may be, do not allow yourself to fall into any trap that would not allow you to dream big and succeed in whichever endeavor you should choose.

Be sure to take a holistic approach to success. In other words, do not measure success by only one criterion, such as material possession, wealth, or power. The pursuit of such is worthy as long as it is qualified and measured against other criteria that indicate personal success (character, industriousness,

---

9   Allen, James, 1910, "As a man Thinketh", Tribecca Books
10 *Return to Love* by Marianne Williamson, Harper Collins, 1992

discipline, etc.….the ABCs that will make you the great person that you were created to be).

The world often measures success in material possessions, wealth or power, but be very careful to understand that this should not be the primary basis you use to measure success.

There are many examples throughout history of people who were very wealthy but certainly not successful at the game of life. By the world's standard, Napoleon Bonaparte was a very successful individual with wealth and power as a result of his military prowess, yet most accounts describe him as a tyrant. Be very careful about the criteria you choose to measure your success and be aware that the criteria you use will dictate the legacy you will leave on this world, as your words and actions most assuredly influence those around you.

I want to be very clear here: it is admirable and honorable to work hard to provide a quality life for yourself and your family, to plan a future built on solid financial planning, and to enjoy life as a result of your hard work and planning. Do not listen to the council of anyone who would encourage you to do otherwise. However, this should not be the desire that trumps all else at the expense of others. There is no amount of wealth worth forfeiting honor, respect for others, and self-respect. A good name is more valuable than gold.

"Dishonest money dwindles away, but whoever gathers money little by little makes it grow." Proverbs 13:11

"A good name is more desirable than great riches; to be esteemed is better than silver or gold." Proverbs 22:1

"For what does it profit a man to gain the whole world, and forfeit his soul?" Mark 8:36

As you create a vision for yourself, make sure it is balanced, serving yourself, serving those around you, and serving the world. Life is about balance. Nature itself proves this point. For example, eating is required for physical survival. Exercise is important as well for physical health and so is a certain amount of rest. One could conclude, therefore, that eating, exercise and rest are important to health, yet without the knowledge that a proper balance of these three critical activities is important, one could cause harm or even death as a result of participating in any of these activities in excess.

For example, if someone sat around eating 24-7, it is safe to say that this activity would result in obesity, which would lead to many health issues. If someone exercised 24-7, certain deaths would occur as a result of malnutrition or exhaustion. Finally, if someone slept 24-7, muscles in the body would experience atrophy, and the efficiency of organs to perform their necessary role toward well-being would begin to decline, ultimately shutting down due to limited activity ultimately leading to death. While this example may seem silly, it perfectly illustrates the importance of balance.

Balance is critical to living life to the fullest and experiencing all that life has to give to us as we live out this human experience. Since a human being is a spiritual being having a physical experience with an intellect, it would be safe to conclude that a balance between spirit, body, and mind is required for the healthy existence of a human being.[11]

When you decide what it is that you really want in life, maintain a consistent balance of spirit, mind and body, get a clear picture of that objective and don't allow any obstacles to throw you off the path. If it doesn't line up with the health of these three human components, it is hazardous at worst and meaningless at best.

"First say to yourself what you want to be; then do what you have to do." Epictetus Greek Philosopher

---

[11] Born Rich workbook page 7, Bob Proctor. Bob Proctor Life Success Productions

Imagine for a moment that you have arrived at the airport, gone through security measures, ventured through the concourse, through the boarding gate, settled into your seat and just prior to take off, the captain welcomes you aboard and announces that he has no idea the destination of the flight. He is simply going to take off, fly for a while, and land the plane at an airport yet undetermined, hopefully before the airplane runs out of fuel.

While there are those "adventurous" people who would be thrilled with the joy of experiencing the unknown, most of us would not be happy as a passenger on a plane without a specific destination. As a matter of fact, most of us would ask to deboard the plane and find a flight that would get us to our desired destination....probably not on the same airline.

Yes, it would be silly for an airline to operate in such a manner, and it would most certainly lead to the failure of the business. It would also be silly for you and I to operate in such a manner. If we have no idea where we are headed, how will we know when we get there? Chances are our plane will never leave the tarmac. So, where do you want to go? What is your objective? Do you have a clear objective? Do you have a specific destination clearly outlined, which spells out who you are, what you are, and what you want to accomplish in your lifetime? If you do not, stop reading right now and choose a specific destination for yourself that promotes health in the areas of spirit, mind and body, serving you and those around you.

Once you have settled on what it is you want in life, once again, it is critical to get a clear mental picture. Allow that picture to soak into your being by diligently practicing mental visualization of the exact "replica" of the desire as if it were already in your possession. Let's use a material possession as an example since it will be easily understood and illustrated. Let's say that one of your objectives to is have a particular new vehicle. Develop a clear mental picture of yourself sitting in the seat of that particular vehicle as you travel happily down the road. As you drive, you cannot help but notice how comfortable the seats are, how smooth the ride is, or how clear the sound system is, but you certainly enjoy the distinctive fragrance of a new vehicle. You find yourself completely satisfied.

A clear vision of our destination is not only powerful but also critical. Can you imagine a professional basketball player waddling down the court in a live basketball game with a blindfold draped across their eyes? It would be absurd to expect the player to place the basketball in a goal that he or she cannot see. Just as it is critical for the basketball player to have a clear vision of the goal in order to score consistently, it is critical for you to have a clear vision of your goal and your destination in life.

"Where there is no vision, the people perish." Proverbs 29:18

Growing up in rural Alabama had its advantages and its disadvantages. There was no movie theater to walk to, no skating rink or no bowling alley, but there was the great outdoors. Living in and experiencing the great outdoors would influence my life more than anything else. I still love the freedom of nature and have fond memories of past experiences.

The Hunt

One of those experiences was hunting. Hunting was an important part of the culture I grew up in. Passed down from generation to generation, evolving from an activity necessary for survival to a favorite past time, hunting was a huge cultural experience. It was so important that my Dad, who was Superman, Spiderman, and Zeus, all rolled up in one to me, purchased a Remington Sportsman 20 gage shotgun for his favorite son (his only son), who was about 2 years old at the time.

For those of you who have the vision of a two-year-old toting around a 20-gage shotgun in rural Alabama, allow me to "clean up" your vision. Yes, my Dad purchased a 20-gage shotgun for me when I was 2 years old, but no, I did not tote it around at age two. As a matter of fact, I couldn't touch it until my Dad determined I was old enough and responsible enough to handle a firearm. I could only dream of the experience of hunting with my very own Remington Sportsman 20 gage and finally, that day came.

While all of the experience is not etched in my memory, there are details that are hard to forget about the experience. Needless to say, I was extremely excited to finally get to go on a quail hunt with my Superman, Spiderman, and Zeus father. I would finally get the chance to prove to him that my training had paid off and that I was indeed the next generation of great hunters. He would be so proud.

The initial excitement wore off quickly after trekking through every briar patch in what seemed to be within 100 miles. Exhausted and bleeding profusely from every exposed and some unexposed areas of my body, I was extremely disappointed that our prized bird dog, Herman, had not located a covey of quail so I could show off my polished shooting skills.

I had three shells locked, loaded, and ready. I had dreamed of this moment. I had dreamed of the moment when my Dad would express how proud he was of his son, who methodically bagged 3 quail with 3 shots. I had even dreamed about bagging 2 quail with one shot, as I had seen my Dad do on occasion. With every briar patch, every step and every drop of blood, the dream was nearing nightmare status……and then, Herman pointed.

I still remember my Dad's voice, woe Herman, woe, as he instructed the prized bird dog not to flush the covey of quail until we were in position. It was a surreal moment. My heart was beating out of my chest with excitement and anticipation as we slowly approached Herman who was obeying my Dad's instructions. It couldn't have been a more perfect situation and then the explosion occurred.

The covey of quail exploded from the ground into the air in front of us. One moment, quiet, peaceful anticipation followed by what sounded like thunder as the covey of quail flushed. Anyone who has ever experienced a flushing covey of quail knows exactly what I am talking about. My excitement had boiled over to a mixture of terror and chaos in an instant.

Instinctively, I began to raise my trusted Remington Sportsman shotgun toward my shoulder as I had been instructed, but that is where my actions based on instruction ended. Before the gun reached my shoulder and well before I had taken careful aim at the quarry, all three shells had been dispensed haphazardly into trees, briars, bushes, and anything else that happened to be at the wrong place at the wrong time. You must be thinking, did a quail happen to be in the wrong place at the wrong time? The answer to that is no.

I have often wondered if my Dad even knew about how disastrous my debut as the next-generation hunter was. If he did, he never expressed it to me. One thing is for sure: it was a memorable experience for me.

There are many things to take away from this experience and this true story. Probably the most obvious thing to learn is to make sure you are standing behind the inexperienced hunter as the covey of quail explodes into the air or perhaps the importance of hunter training courses that were nonexistent in that era.

The thing I want to illustrate from this experience is the importance of a clear vision. It is easy to dream about an experience, but the likelihood of experiencing something worthwhile is much greater, beginning with vision followed by proper planning and action. Just like the hunt, you can't hit what you can't see. The difference between the dreamer and the achiever begins with a clear vision of the thing you wish to achieve or the thing you wish to possess.

We think in a series of pictures. To illustrate this, think for a moment about the home you live in and notice that instantly, a picture of the home you live in pops onto the screen of your mind. Think about a good friend or family member and boom, a picture of this individual immediately appears in your mind; there is no disputing it.

Since we have established the fact that we think in pictures, we could likewise establish the fact that it is important to be careful what we think about. It is true; stinkin' thinkin' leads to stinkin' results. Worthwhile thoughts lead to worthwhile results.

Since we think in pictures, you are doing nothing more than intentionally thinking about your desire and practicing the visual image in your mind, enhancing the picture with each practice. Every man-made thing that exists in the world today was once nothing more than a thought. See only the objective and all obstacles will give way.

> *"The most pathetic person is the person who has sight but no vision." Helen Keller*

Avoid the practice of being "scatterbrained," where pictures of numerous "things" flash upon the theatre of the mind. In this case, your attention is so diluted that it becomes impossible to acquire anything of particular significance, thus exhausting your efforts in the sporadic pursuit of nothing. Worse than this, if we are not careful, the things we think about (visualize) are the exact opposite of the very thing we desire, giving us exactly what we have focused on, the thing that we do not want. Therefore, choose your thoughts wisely, precisely and intentionally. Proper thought, proper vision directs our attention toward proper things that produce proper fruit in our life.

> *"Keep your eyes focused on what is right: Look straight ahead to what is good." Proverbs 4:25*

What is it that you want from this life? If your life were perfect, what would it look like? What would be the specific details of this perfect life? Don't read any further until you have answered these questions for yourself. Once you have answered these questions, see only the objective so clearly that all obstacles must give way.

Before you can do something, you must be something. Do you clearly see only the objective? I do.

I am Passionate about this life and the way that I live it

The gift of life is immeasurably precious. The very incredible odds of a particular human's existence should be enough to warrant daily thanksgiving. The existence of each human being is possible only by the existence of a mother and father whose existence was possible as a result of the survival of each partner from generation after generation through the beginning of man's existence. Confused? Let's simplify by asking a couple of questions.

What if one (it only takes one) of your descendants had suffered a life-ending event resulting in one of the many plagues that have wiped out thousands upon thousands throughout history just prior to playing their part in the procreation of the descendant in your genealogical past? The life-ending event could be a result of any number of things, such as war, disease, natural causes, accidents, you name it. The premature death of that or any other descendent for any reason would have nullified your existence. When you consider all of the possibilities for nonexistence, the odds are insurmountable. You and I are very fortunate to be blessed with this precious gift of life.

Why then is it that so many people take their lives for granted as if it has no value? Why do so many people waste their lives through dependency on a drug, another person, a government, or a material thing? Why do so many people waste precious moments on meaningless activities devoid of passion? Why? The answer is simple. They place no value on their life.

Life is precious, much too precious to waste. Each individual was created uniquely different and for a specific purpose. There are no two people alike. Identical twins may appear to be the same by visual appearance, but they are two unique individuals.

There has never been nor will there ever be another you. You will always have critics but understand this: You are special and the life that you have been given is a precious gift so be passionate about your life and the way you live it. You were created to do great things, not mediocre things. Everyone cannot be the President of the United States of America but that doesn't mean you cannot be great.

As mentioned before and worth mentioning again, the measure of greatness is not measured by the level of accomplishment; it is measured by the level of accomplishment based on the ability you possess. Mother Theresa didn't have many material possessions when she passed away, but she lived a life of great accomplishment. She used the ability to love others, see through their mental, spiritual or physical debilitated state, and see the value of human life. By being passionate about the life she was given, she not only served the individuals she cared for but also inspired a world full of dysfunctional, selfish, and sometimes evil people. Mother Theresa didn't spend her precious gift of life; she invested it to accomplish the seemingly impossible, always selflessly reaching out with passion to change the world for the better.

> *"Every great dream begins with a dreamer. Always remember you have within you the strength, the patience and the passion to reach for the stars to change the world."* Harriet Tubman[12]

Perhaps you have taken the gift of life for granted. Perhaps you could even conclude that you have wasted the time you have been given thus far and therefore, you have failed miserably. After you get through feeling sorry for yourself for failing or wasting your life, pick yourself up off the mat, understand that everyone fails and has wasted precious moments of life, and get about the business of living life with passion. Don't waste another precious moment. Be about the business of living life to the fullest NOW!

To live life to the fullest requires passion not only for life itself but in the way you live it. Be passionate as a spouse, a parent, a child, a sibling, a coworker, an employee or a friend. When one is passionate, they exhibit strong feelings or enthusiasm towards that which they are passionate about. How could one not exhibit strong feelings or enthusiasm about being alive?

If you want to have a good life, be passionate about life by exhibiting strong feelings and enthusiasm toward the daily activities of life and the precious gift of life itself. It is easy to fall into a "rut," doing one meaningless thing after another, day after day. Be careful about allowing yourself to get into a rut. The definition of a rut as it pertains to living is a grave with the ends kicked out. Get out of the rut and start living.

We have all found ourselves stuck in a rut from time to time. Those moments in life when it seems everything we do "goes south." It is okay to get in a rut from time to time; as a matter of fact, you can expect it. It's not ok to stay there.

Growing up on a farm in rural Alabama has afforded me the opportunity to find myself stuck on numerous occasions. I have experienced the "Joy" of

---

12   Brainy Quote

sticking trucks, tractors, ATVs, bulldozers, track-hoes, backhoes, combines, etc. You name it and I have probably had it stuck.

There are two things consistent about my experience of getting stuck on the farm, the first of which is obvious: I am somewhere that I shouldn't be. If you want to find yourself stuck in a rut, just go somewhere you shouldn't be and you will find yourself there whether physically or mentally. Mixing with the wrong crowd will get you there physically just like stinkin' thinking will get you there mentally. Being passionate about the precious gift of life will steer you away from the hazards of being in a rut.

The second thing consistent about my experience of being stuck on the farm is that I don't stay there. It would be foolish to abandon a vehicle or piece of equipment simply because it was stuck in a rut. The vehicle or piece of machinery is recovered by any means necessary because it is too valuable to remain idle. Your life, too, is much too valuable to remain stuck in a rut. Be passionate about this life and the way that you live it.

If you want to have good relationships in your life, be passionate about those relationships, exhibiting strong feelings and enthusiasm toward those with whom you have relationships with by giving them respect with sincere caring and loving attention that they deserve. If you want to enjoy your chosen career, be passionate about it, and exhibit strong feelings and enthusiasm toward the activities and other people involved in your career.

> ***"Without passion you don't have energy, without energy you have nothing." Donald Trump***

Does that mean that life will always be a thrilling adventure, that relationships will always be respectful, loving, and caring, or that a chosen career will be without challenge? Absolutely not. As a matter of fact, life is difficult, relationships are difficult, and careers are difficult. All things of value come with a certain degree of difficulty. Usually the greater the value, the greater the degree of difficulty.

> *"Being challenged in life is inevitable. Being defeated is optional." Roger Crawford*

Expect difficulty to exist but look at difficulty as an opportunity for personal growth. As a muscle requires resistance for growth, so is resistance required for personal growth. When the challenges and difficulties of life are looked upon as an opportunity rather than a setback, the effort required to overcome the challenges and difficulties is more readily available to come to your aid. A setback is a setup for a comeback. Since being passionate about life and the way it is lived requires strong feelings and enthusiasm, difficulty and resistance are no match for anyone who has chosen (there is that word again) to be passionate about life and the way it is lived.

Begin now to make it a habit to appreciate the precious gift of life in the good times and bad. As you ride the waves of life, choose the direction your rudder will be pointed in. Set sail toward the things of life that expose the inner passion hidden below the surface of your being that allow you to be the best you can be thus leaving a legacy of strong feeling and enthusiasm to a world and a people in much need of such a thing. Be passionate about life and the way you live it.

Before you can do something, you must be something.

I understand there are times when I need to be Quiet

Oh, my goodness. I need to read this, re-read it, and read it again. It is so not easy to do. While there is a time to speak, there is also a time to be quiet. Some occasions to be quiet include listening in order to learn something important, avoiding conflict by "taking the high road," and avoiding showing your ignorance of a particular subject or situation.

An individual who lives life with passion must have a certain degree of its polar opposite, that of being quiet. As a top has a bottom, a left has a right, an inside has an outside and a beginning has an end so it is that passion requires a degree of reservation, which is implemented by being quiet. One cannot exist without the other, nor can an individual expect good things to happen in their life without knowing when to be passionate and when to be quiet.

"A fool gives full vent to his spirit but a wise man quietly holds it back." Proverbs 29:11

Knowing when to be quiet is a valuable tool to have in the tool chest. It is a tool that exists in the tool chest of every successful person who ever lived. Many conflicts could have been avoided by simply practicing the art of being quiet, and many a fool's true colors have been exposed by words that flow freely and without thought, spoken recklessly for anyone and everyone to hear. Learning to open your ears and close your mouth will take you far in life.

> *"Those who guard their lips preserve their lives, but those who speak rashly will come to ruin." Proverbs 13:3*

So, how do you learn to do that? Through disciplined practice, you learn to be quiet the same way you learned how to speak, tie your shoes, ride a bicycle, or walk. Before your mouth opens to speak, be wise to guard your tongue by practicing the activity of giving thought to the words poised to flow from you. Once the words are spoken, it is too late to take them back. The harm caused is instantaneous, and the birth of conflict is not only inevitable but often irreversible. Anyone and everyone has had experiences when the intentional practice of giving thought to speech would have served them well.

I can think of a number of times when I made the emotional decision to speak my mind. Each of these occasions is a reminder that emotional decisions are usually not good decisions. In other words, I wish I would have kept my mouth shut, but once the words roll off of your lips, they are spoken. Unfortunately, there is no redo in the world of communication. On each occasion, I knew as soon as the words left my mouth, I knew they served no purpose other than to put on full display for all to see, or in this case, hear, a full dose of my ignorance.

For the most part, I now mostly sit back and listen to others. I have certainly learned that there is a time to speak and a time to be quiet and that, most often, time should be spent being quiet instead of speaking.

On occasion, when you are in the presence of others, be aware of the opportunity to "stick your foot in your mouth" and avoid conflict by simply being quiet at appropriate times. Giving sufficient thought to your words should provide the proper discretion as to when to stand your ground and when to simply be quiet and walk away.

Pick your battles wisely, as you will have opportunities for many. Trouble often comes looking for the unsuspecting individual, thus leaving them vulnerable and leading to a reaction rather than a response. A reaction occurs when one gives little or no thought toward action, including speech. A response is a well-thought-out action or lack of action, which would include speech or the lack of speech (being quiet). Start by understanding that there are times when you need to be quiet.

The area between being passionate and being quiet can sometimes be gray, but most often, it is black and white. Let's discuss a few.

Rule number one. Never speak out of anger. Anger is an emotion that most often clouds our judgement. I cannot think of a time when I spoke out of anger and the result was positive. Divorce, murder, slander, and world conflicts began on the premise of words spoken out of anger. Avoid anger if possible, but avoid angry speech at all costs.

Avoid the practice of an age-old pastime, gossip. I suppose gossip has been around since the beginning of time. Nothing can perk our ears quicker than juicy gossip. Perhaps it brings comfort when we hear of someone else who has failed in one way or another, thus smoothing over our misgivings or perhaps our desire to participate in juicy gossip elevates our status by proving to others that we are not "that bad". Whatever the reason, gossip is unproductive at best and usually proves destructive to ourselves or someone else; therefore, be quiet.

If you don't have knowledge of a particular subject, be quiet. Nothing sounds more foolish than someone talking about something they know nothing about.

We all know the guy or gal who is an expert about everything. They can explain in detail everything that you are doing wrong and why their way is better. I mentioned earlier that I had such an experience in a sales training program where we "paired up" to practice selling a product. We were instructed to take turns as the salesperson to sell a particular product to our "paired up" partner.

When my partner finished his sales pitch, as I had been instructed, I shared with him a couple of minor things that I thought he could improve on. By the time he finished telling me how wrong my analysis was, followed by his scathing critique of my sales pitch, I was almost convinced that I had made a major mistake by choosing to leave a good-paying job to take a position where failure was certainly imminent.

While his words did make me feel uncomfortable and, for a moment, made me question my validity as a salesperson, thank goodness I didn't dwell on them. Before the end of the year, he was gone, and I was awarded the 2nd runner-up Rookie Award from the company, which was the first of many awards to follow as well as many years of successful service.

I can honestly say that I did not find joy in his failure, nor am I prideful about my accomplishments. I chose to share the story because the experience was one of many that proved there is a time to be quiet. When you don't know what you are talking about, it is one of those times.

Despite the best intentions, do not share information from an unreliable source or information based on nonfactual evidence. In the US justice system, a guilty plea is reached when the prosecution team has proven guilt beyond a reasonable doubt to a jury based on facts, whether through reliable witnesses or solid evidence. Hearsay and wishy-washy evidence is not admissible in court, nor is it used to determine the guilt of a defendant. While there are cases of wrongful convictions, most cases are properly handled through solid, reliable evidence, and each jury member is charged with the responsibility of applying evidence without bias.

Consider yourself a jury member. We live in a society of information overload, so you will come across multiple sources of information, and you must be responsible not only for how you process information but also for how you share information. Intelligent, successful people communicate based on facts. If you don't have information based on facts, do yourself and others a big favor, be quiet.

Always remember that there is power in words but perhaps more importantly, remember that there is power in keeping quiet. Words can be used for good or bad. Make sure the words you speak bring about good. Know when to speak but also know when to be quiet.

Before you can do something, you must be something. Have you learned that there are times when it is best to be quiet? I have.

I am Resilient in my pursuit of continuous improvement

One thing is for sure. You are either moving forward or moving backward, there is no such thing as sitting still. To be complacent or non-engaged in the direction of your life is likened to getting in a vehicle, putting it in reverse and hitting the accelerator, all the while looking straight ahead to see where you are not going. Continuous improvement in all areas of life is necessary for growth. It is imperative in order to live life to the fullest and enjoy the results.

> *"Life is a gift and it offers us the privilege, opportunity and responsibility to give something back by becoming more."*
> *Anthony Robbins*

Everyone should ask themselves, "What could I dare to achieve?" Often, a person will achieve very little in a lifetime because the task at hand seems enormous and unobtainable or as we spoke of earlier, they never set a destination. As a result, very little or no effort is expended toward the accomplishment of anything. When we find ourselves in this condition of thought, it is imperative to change our way of thinking.

When we find ourselves overwhelmed, instead of trying to "bite off more than we can chew" by measuring the entire task, we should measure it piece by piece or day by day. Break the task down into smaller, manageable portions.

Think of the task as a pie. What is the best way to eat a pie? One bite at a time, right? How about climbing a mountain? We don't leap to the top of the mountain; we climb it. Climbing any mountain, whether a physical mountain or a mountainous task, is successfully climbed one step at a time. Focus on each step, not the mountain. Focusing on the mountain can prove to be intimidating, but by keeping your head down and focusing on each step along the way, the mountain is climbed.

To achieve anything of greatness requires a continuous sustained effort day after day or piece by piece or step by step in terms of eating pies and climbing mountains. Piece by piece, task by task, phone call by phone call, step by step, minute by minute, day by day, week by week, month by month, and year by year are required for success. Rome was not built in a day, nor will your success happen in a day.

There is no such thing as an overnight success. The professional musician spent hour after hour, day after day, week after week, and year after year refining their talent until they finally got their big break. The professional athlete spent hour after hour, day after day, week after week, month after month, and year after year developing the skills to perform at a high level in order to make the team. Certainly, a degree of natural God-given ability is required, but there are numerous examples of people with God-given talent in any walk of life standing on the sidelines or in the stands as a spectator watching many less gifted "Go-getters" excel as a result of their relentless pursuit of excellence.

How many times have you heard someone say, "I am going to do that," or "I want to be this," or "I wish I had that"? I have heard it from people all of my life, mostly from people who never accomplish anything of significance because they spend their time and energy envying what others have rather than making the required effort to get it themselves.

The world doesn't serve the "gonna-doers," the "wannabe's" or those who wish their life away. The people who get ahead, who make a contribution to the world, who make something out of nothing are the doers! The top 10% of the doers are in resilient pursuit of continuous improvement. They are always looking for more efficient and effective ways of making themselves and those around them better.

> *"Those who work their land will have abundant food, but those who chase fantasies will have their fill of poverty."*
> *Proverbs 28:19*

Another way of thought is to think of your pursuit of continuous improvement being similar to that of a financial investment. When someone makes a financial investment, they expect a return. The return may seem very minuscule in the short term, but in the long term, compounding of interest will amass a very favorable "nest egg." For instance, a $20 per week investment at a conservative 5% gain over a 40-year period of time would result in a sum of $131,913. A small investment totaling $41,600 spread out over 40 years with a small percentage of growth yields an amount in excess of 3 times the total investment. This is the concept of compound interest.

For the financial investment, simple math proves that either a larger investment or a higher rate of return provides a greater yield. Similarly, a larger time/effort investment in an endeavor you are pursuing will provide a greater yield. An investment of time/effort into a worthy cause (higher rate of return) will provide a greater yield.

And so it is with personal growth investment. Invest a little every day toward continuous improvement and watch it grow. The compounding interest works the same way for personal growth as it does for a monetary investment. The more you put in, the more you get out. Just as an apple a day keeps the doctor away, $20 per week will result in a nice return over time. An investment in the most important thing in the world, Y O U, will pay dividends towards a bright future.

Be aware that every "investment" will not always yield the desired return. As a matter of fact, just like the financial markets, an investment sometimes loses value in the form of disappointment. Let those disappointments roll off of your back like water rolls off a duck's back.

Expect good times and disappointments to be interwoven into the fiber of life. Being aware of this fact will be critical preparation when the challenges of life occur. When those challenges occur, be like the old ship's captain weathering the storm, steady as she goes, continuing on toward your destination.

Find the thing in life that really brings you joy (high rate of return), be relentless in your pursuit of mastering whatever it is (time/effort), and begin the journey towards its accomplishment. Be realistic, but be aggressive. For example, it wouldn't matter how much I wanted to be a football player in the NFL or how hard I worked to make a team; I am well past the age of having the physical capabilities to accomplish such a thing. On the other hand, just because something seems "out of reach" doesn't mean that you shouldn't pursue it.

Once you find the thing that really brings you joy, invest the proper time and training to become the best there is. Setting your goals high allows you a little "wiggle room" in the event you fall short. A friend of mine once said, "When you shoot for the moon and miss, you still land among the stars." This is good advice for those seeking continuous improvement.

There are a few practical things that you can do to make continuous improvements. These practical things are easy and enjoyable.

First and foremost, surround yourself with other positive people who are also resilient in their pursuit of continuous improvement. Perhaps you have heard, "If you hang out with dogs, you will get fleas." In other words, a sure recipe for failure and heartache is to surround yourself with people of low morale value or self-worth.

This does not mean that you should have a "holier than thou" attitude towards people who make bad decisions. If that were the case, there would be no one to hang out with because we all make bad decisions. There are those people, however, who never learn from their bad decisions and there are even those whose purpose in life is to selfishly live by their rules with no regard to how it affects anyone else. Stay away from these bad apples.

Instead, surround yourself with bright, energetic people who have a clear purpose that will serve the world and are interested in getting better each day. Become better by feeding off of the energy emitted by these individuals and choose to make those around you better by simply being around you. Bring out the best in others while they do the same for you.

Second of all, spend time reading, studying, and learning about things that can improve your life. There are millions of books written about specific subjects waiting to be read by you and countless others. To become a master chef requires study and practice. I enjoy eating food prepared by someone with superior culinary skills. They have studied and practiced to learn just exactly which ingredients and the measure of such ingredients to bring enjoyment to the palate. Read, study and learn about the things that will make you the master chef of your life.

Create specific daily activities that will bring improvement to your life. One thing I have found that helps me experience continuous improvement is the memorization of scripture and quotes. Without the luxury of time due to a busy schedule I choose to keep it simple. If I can memorize one scripture a week along with one quote, I am making continuous improvement.

This simple exercise has produced great results. I couldn't begin to count the number of times I have faced a challenge, big or small, that a quote or a scripture has helped me focus on "the big picture" instead of the circumstance.

Find something simple that you can implement into your daily schedule that will bring improvement into your life. Just like the mountain that you climbed step by step, the heights reached through daily activities of improvement have made your footsteps firm on the mountain, giving you the vision to see over the circumstances of life. Your focus is, therefore, on the things that matter rather than the circumstances or the things that do not matter.

Dream big or live small. Leave it all on the field. Live in a manner that when the end of your days are drawing near it is impossible to look back and wish there were something you would have done. The choice is yours whether you will be disappointed or fulfilled by that which you have accomplished. Make it a sure thing by being resilient in your pursuit of continuous improvement.

Are you investing wisely in yourself? Do you have a plan for continuous growth? Be accountable to yourself, to those that you care about and to those that care about you by being resilient in your pursuit of continuous improvement.

Before you can do something, you must be something. I am resilient in my pursuit of continuous improvement. Are you?

I am a Servant to others

I can still remember well the exhilaration of Christmas I experienced as a child. My sister and I could hardly go to sleep on Christmas Eve due to the anticipation of gifts that would magically appear under the Christmas tree, waiting to be enjoyed. The Christmas wish list had been spoken, I had not been naughty (at least I hadn't been caught being naughty), everyone was full from dinner, the leftovers were parked in the refrigerator and we were snugly tucked into bed. After a full night of sleep or a little nap, if actual sleep time were recorded, the moment that had been anticipated for 365 days had finally arrived. It was time to receive our gifts! It was amazing that Santa Claus knew just exactly what it would take to put a huge smile on my face.

While those times were special, the true joy of Christmas transitions from receiving gifts to giving gifts. The joy of putting a smile on the face of someone you love and care about on Christmas Day or any other day is immeasurable. There is joy in serving others!

Of course, we shouldn't wait for the holiday of Christmas to serve others. Every day should be Christmas. Make it a point to seek out at least one person to serve every day.

You don't have to look far to find opportunities to serve. We are surrounded by people who are in need nearly every day of our lives. When we approach people as if they are hurting and in need, I believe we are right 80 – 90 percent of the time. The world is full of hurting people.

There are some misconceptions about serving other people. Let's identify a few of these misconceptions so we don't miss the joy of serving because we don't understand them.

First of all, serving others does not require money. Oftentimes, since we live in a society that places so much emphasis on money, we tend to believe that serving others requires money. Certainly, money can be used to serve others and if you have it, you should use it in such a manner, but there are many other ways to serve others. Unto much is given, much is expected.

Serving others also does not require a lot of time, which is our "go-to" excuse. Go ahead and put "I don't have time" back in your excuse bag for something else. There is no place for it as it pertains to serving others.

Some acts of service, such as a mission trip or visiting a loved one or friend in need, do require time, but there are many opportunities for service that fall right into our daily routines. Serving others can be as simple as holding the door open at a place of business, or smiling at an approaching individual on a sidewalk, placing an encouraging phone call or sending a little note to someone who needs a word of encouragement or hope. None of these acts of service require a great allotment of time. They only require an allotment of action on our part.

This type of service can be contagious. I love the commercial that illustrates random acts of service similar to those above and how it prompts the recipient to reciprocate by performing an act of service on someone else's behalf. We never know the impact of our service on a broken world. Change your part of the world by serving others. As you can see, it doesn't have to cost time or money, but it will pay dividends to your soul through the smiles placed on the faces of others by simply showing them that you care about them.

Another misconception of a servant is that servants are weak and are, therefore, used by stronger people. That misconception is far from the truth. To the contrary, being served is easy and therefore obtainable by the weakest among us. To be a servant requires mental strength and in some cases, physical strength. If you have the belief that you are too good to be a servant, then you will surely live a miserable existence, being served only by yourself.

The most memorable act of service that I have experienced took place at the Atlanta airport several years ago. My wife Kathy and I were grabbing a bite to eat while we were waiting to board a plane headed for Ireland. The food court and surrounding corridors were occupied to a large degree by US military personnel who had been deployed and were awaiting flights to Iraq.

As I stood in line to place my order, I could not help but think about the service men and women that surrounded Kathy and I. Here we were headed out on a bucket list destination and there they were headed out to a foreign battlefield to fight for my country and my freedom, willing to give their lives for both. The moment was overwhelming.

As we neared the counter, the serviceman in front of us began to place his order. Out of pure instinct, I told the serviceman to order whatever he wanted and that I was paying for it. After we had both placed our orders and paid for the meals, we carried on a brief conversation.

All I remember from our conversation is that he was from New York and he thanked me for buying his meal. I literally fought the tears back as I said, "No, thank you for your service." My emotions would not allow any more words to come out of my mouth, so we went our separate ways. It was a powerful moment, so powerful that I kept the receipt.

I didn't keep the receipt so that I could look back and pat myself on the shoulder for my service; I kept it as a reminder to me how powerful it is when we serve others. In the same sense, I don't tell this story so others will think that I am all that for buying a meal for a serviceman; I tell it to share with others that there is power in serving others. **Don't miss out on the joy of serving others.**

The reality of the situation was that his sacrifice of service to our country was magnified greatly in terms of my service to purchase a meal for him from a fast-food restaurant. The soldier has probably long forgotten the moment, but I will never forget the power of that moment for me.

No matter how large or small our service to others is, there is power in it, power for the recipient and power in the server. You never know how an act of service could change a life. As you go about your day, be aware of those around and seek out ways to serve them. I heard someone tell me something that I will never forget. When we approach another individual, we should approach them as if they are hurt because nine times out of ten, they are. I don't remember where I heard this, but it is true. There are a lot of hurting people in our world, people who are waiting for someone like you to send a blessing their way. Be a blessing today!

Before you can do something, you must be something. Are you a servant to others? I am.

I am Truthful with myself and others

To be honest and trustworthy is a worthy and noble calling in a world that makes it so easy to be deceptive and manipulative in order to "get ahead." Deceptive and manipulative practices are common in the business and personal lives of many without any regard for the well-being of others. Success is never found at the expense of another. It is found only in service to others by being honest and trustworthy.

> *"Honesty and integrity are absolutely essential for success in life - all areas of life. The really good news is that anyone can develop both honesty and integrity."* Zig Ziglar

> *"What a person desires is unfailing love; better to be poor than a liar." Proverbs 19:22*

Honesty today is in short supply. I am amazed at how dishonest some people can be. I mentioned politicians earlier. Not all, but many of our elected officials are downright dishonest. What may be more sad than their dishonesty is that they are rarely held accountable. It is as if once you are elected to public office, you have a free pass to be dishonest. On top of that, the media tells lies (disinformation about disinformation). I believe it is a picture of the state of our society.

I can remember a day when honor through honesty was a cornerstone of civil society. You could count on most people to be truthful. At least if they were caught in their dishonesty, they had remorse.

My wife is an elementary school teacher. To date, she has given 31 years of service to public education. I couldn't do it myself, but I believe being an educator is one of the most honorable of professions, especially public educators who deal with children who do not always have the best of home lives.

Obviously, we talk about our professions on a regular basis, so I know what is going on in education. What is going on in education is alarming. The gage of moral character in education has taken a nose dive in the last 31 years. Parents, students, and yes, sometimes educator's morals are on the decline. Why is that? There are certainly many reasons for the decline, but I believe one of the underlying reasons is that our society has made it common to justify our declining behavior, especially in regards to honesty. We have come up with terms like "white lies" to somehow justify being dishonest. Society's dishonesty has progressed to the point that we are attempting to rewrite history books to fit a particular narrative. That is another story for another day but hopefully, you get the point. Dishonesty is accepted.

I could write a gazillion pages about the subject, but I prefer to focus on the solution to the problem. *The solution is you and me.* **We are the answer to the problem.** We must be consistent with our determination to be honest. It needs to be who we are. We need to teach our children and their children.

I love to eat blackberry cobbler. Obviously, one of the key ingredients in a blackberry cobbler is blackberries. Without the blackberries, it is easy to determine that it is impossible to have a blackberry cobbler. It is not hard to figure that out, right? Similarly, one of the key ingredients to being a complete human being is honesty. There is no more admired attribute in a person than that of honesty. You can always count on an honest person to do the right thing despite the circumstances. You will always be treated properly by an honest person.

The Golden Rule, "Do unto others what you would have them do unto you," is very applicable in this case. Certainly, no one appreciates being lied to, nor does anyone have any respect for a liar. Just think of a person that you know of; we all have them in our lives, who is a habitual liar. Do you or others have any respect for that person? Is that the type of reputation that you would desire for yourself? Of course not. To be held in high esteem requires honesty.

> ***Better is a poor man who walks in his integrity than a rich man who is crooked in his ways. Proverbs 28:6***

Practice being an upstanding human being daily. Start with honesty. ***Before you can do something, you must be something***. Are you truthful with yourself and others? I am.

I am Understanding that there are differences among us

Many people throughout the history of mankind have lost their lives as a result of being different, whether culturally, religiously, regionally or simply personally. Conflict has abounded and I suppose it will continue to do so as a result of differences among us.

Our world today is filled with hate based on personal beliefs or biases. It is ok to be different, just as it is okay to be hated for being different, but it is not okay to hate. Hate is such a strong emotion. There is no place for hate in the heart of a person who practices the ABCs of Transformation.

Hatred is a powerful emotion that carries with it negative feelings and thoughts. This emotional baggage weighs down our very soul. When we have hatred in our heart towards another individual, we tend to bargain with ourselves that the other person is the one being hurt by our hatred when, all the while, we are the ones who have unknowingly chosen to carry this unnecessary, unproductive, and certainly unhealthy baggage.

Society has a way of categorizing individuals based on a countless number of criteria. You are white or black, young or old, rich or poor, healthy or non-healthy, religious or non-religious, skinny or fat, smart or not smart, Democrat or Republican, blah, blah, blah, blah, blah…..when in reality WE are all HUMAN BEINGS uniquely created by our creator with precisely desired specifications from and of our creator.

Who am I and who are you, to question the value of a person based on the criteria of simply being different? Understand there are differences among us, accept it, learn to live with it, and move on to more important things. There are bigger fish to fry!

It is imperative to personal and professional success to accept people as they are, learn to work with others, if need be, to accomplish a common goal, and use common sense guidelines to stay on track. It is not my place, your place, or anyone else's place, nor is it my responsibility to judge another person except in the arena of civil justice.

Do not misinterpret this instruction. Your beliefs and values are not to be compromised by keeping company with another whose beliefs and values are not in alignment with yours, nor are these instructions intended to have you in any way change your beliefs or compromise your values. Your beliefs and values are yours to choose from, so be diligent to put plenty of thought into them in order to be deeply rooted.

You should feel no pressure to wander away from your thoughts and beliefs as a result of someone else's beliefs. You are to expect others to respect you and your beliefs and others should expect the same.

You can expect it, but that doesn't mean that you will get it. Chances are, you will be challenged more than once in your lifetime to defend your beliefs, so be prepared to do so through the principles we have discussed. The daily practice through study, fellowship with like-minded people and action, along with respecting those ones who are different, will produce deep roots that will provide a firm foundation upon which to grow and flourish.

When the winds of adversity and or temptation blow hard toward you, your deep-rooted beliefs and values hold strong and keep you grounded in what you know to be true because you have prepared. Understand and hold tight to the precept that while it is acceptable for others to be different than you, it is also acceptable for you to be different than others. Therefore, place utmost urgency in determining for yourself specifically what those beliefs are.

The purpose and general instruction of this entire manuscript is for you to know who you are, what you are and why, which can only be accomplished through much thought and preparation. Your success as an individual will be based on your actions toward this very important activity. If you are not willing to do that for yourself, someone else would be glad to do it for you, and you can be certain that they will put their interests before yours.

> *"My son, do not walk in the way with them; hold back your foot from their paths." Proverbs 1:15*

Be aware and accept that there are people all around who share different beliefs, look different, talk differently, and walk differently. The uniqueness of each of us as human beings is what makes everyone special in our own right since we are all created by our creator exactly the way our creator intended. Our creator had a perfect design in mind. After all, he is the creator, so he knew exactly what he was doing. He knew if everyone were exactly the same, life would be boring and unfulfilling.

The quicker you embrace and accept the fact that we are all different in our appearance, thoughts, beliefs, and actions, the better off you will be. Understand that there are differences among us.

It doesn't take long for a married couple to determine that there are differences between husband and wife that weren't noticeable during the engagement. Coworkers share differences of opinions as to how the job should be done. Church members disagree over things like what the color of the carpet should be when it is time to replace it.

Do yourself a favor. Dwell on the things about your spouse that you love rather than the differences among you and you will have a happy marriage. Work hand in hand with your coworkers to get the job done, understanding that your way may not always be right and that you, your coworker, and your employer will all benefit.

Be open-minded rather than narrow-minded when it comes to insignificant things such as the color of the carpet in a church or other organization and you, as well as the church or other organization along with its members, will benefit. Dwelling on such trivial details serves no one.

I was once asked if I would rather have church in the "old sanctuary" or the "new family life center. While I had an opinion, I did not offer it. My answer was, "It doesn't matter to me if we have church in the old church, the new family life center or the parking lot, as long as we have church." There is a time and place to pick a side, but that wasn't one of them. Be wise to "pick your fights" because you will have many choices since there are differences among us.

I cannot emphasize enough how important it is to accept others as they are and how equally important it is to accept yourself despite being different. Being different does not mean that you are of any less value than someone who is "normal," whatever "normal" is, nor is anyone else a lesser person because they are not like us.

Take what you have and run with it! You are uniquely gifted and designed for a purpose. Use the unique gifts that you have to fulfill the purpose planted in your heart while accepting others who were designed for a different purpose.

One other thing. Don't try to force your ways on someone else or publicly criticize them if they do not think the way you do. You be you and let them be them. Social media has made cowards out of many people as they air their differences publicly. I don't know any other way to put it. Nobody cares about that crap! Have the decency to settle your differences privately. Understand that you are not always right. Sometimes, it is best to take the high road and agree to disagree. No two people are alike and no two people think alike. Take a load off of yourself and grasp that. You may be right or you may not be right; either way, take a chill pill and live in peace with your fellow man/woman.

Do you understand that there are differences among us? Are you accepting of all individuals despite differences? Understand that there are differences among us all, and you will find that your relationships, whether personal or professional, will thrive as a result. ***Before you can do something, you must be something***. Be understanding that there are differences among us.

Victory is mine

Victory, sweet victory. We all want to win ….always. Whether it is a card game with friends, an organized sporting event as an athlete or fan or a simple disagreement. It is human nature to want to come out as victor over our rival. There is something special about winning!

Everyone cannot win all the time. Just like there is, a front has a back, a top has a bottom, an in has an out, someone wins and someone loses. That is a good thing. It doesn't always feel that way, but human nature would decide that long before we are born. While winning is exhilarating and necessary for the psych, so losing is also necessary for the psych. I must admit that was hard to put into words because I love to win…..always.

I don't want to admit it, but there are two good things about losing. First of all, while winning has a way of lifting our spirits, it can also lift our ego if we are not careful. Sometimes, we need a little "humble pill," and losing is just what the doctor ordered when it comes to keeping us grounded.

The second thing that losing does for us is it helps us appreciate victory. If we always won at everything, I am certain that we would become complacent and less appreciative of victory.

I have noticed in my life that I need a little sandpaper to go along with "smooth." When everything goes as "smooth as glass," I tend to get complacent, unappreciative and sometimes even bored. The sandpaper has a way of keeping me on my toes, focused on the smooth as glass and action.

OK, so I talked about the necessity of losing. It was difficult, but I did it. Enough of that because, did I mention, I love the win....always!!

I am not the only one who loves to win, always. As a matter of fact, if you don't like to win you should seek professional help. Winning is fantastic!

Sometimes, the urge to be victorious causes people to use bad judgement. Misguided people make a living by implementing, on a daily basis, poor business practices at the expense of unsuspecting customers and consider themselves victorious. Having spent many years in the insurance business, I have seen first-hand people who profited and advanced their careers, taking advantage of the unsuspecting. There is no place for this type of activity. It would be better to be an honest, poor person than it would be to be a rich crook. You can carry dignity to the grave, but riches will stay behind. Even silly disputes or disagreements over ballgames have resulted in injury and even death.

One who practices these types of activities is not to be considered a success. While they perceive themselves as victorious because of their elevated status and while others looking from the outside may perceive themselves as victorious, at the end of the day, they are the biggest losers. As the scripture says, "What good is it to gain the world and lose your soul?"

All of the awards, money, prestige and recognition are not worth sacrificing your character and reputation. There is something to be said for an individual who exercises his or her fiduciary responsibility towards others who have placed their trust in them, relying on them to be treated fairly and appropriately. When an opportunity arises to "take advantage" of another, ask yourself, "Would I do this for my mother?" That is, of course, considering that you love and respect your mother. If your answer is a definitive "yes," go for it.

> ***"The price of victory is high but so are the rewards." Paul Bear Bryant***

To be truly victorious requires a tremendous amount of effort, sacrifice, hard work, and grit. Nothing worthwhile in this life comes easy. The things that really matter, such as strong family relationships, a healthy body, a positive social life, a sharp mind or a strong spiritual life, and a purposeful profession, to name a few, require one to be disciplined enough to exert the effort and do the things required of them to receive such blessings.

For those of you who do not like to pay, I will be happy to present it in another way that will perhaps make you feel good about taking action. Don't think about paying the price; rather, think about reaping the rewards, as Zig Ziglar so eloquently put it in his award-winning audio message "See you at the top."

Zig says, "You don't pay the price for success, you enjoy the benefits of it. You don't pay the price for a good marriage, you reap the benefits of a good marriage. You don't pay the price for good health, you enjoy the benefits of good health". To read it is a great thing, but to hear Zig Ziglar speak these words as only he can is truly fantastic.

Would you rather enjoy the benefits of taking action towards improving these things or pay the price? Plenty of people pay the price for a failing marriage from the checkbook and the soul. Plenty of people pay the price for unhealthy habits, a terrible family life, a dull mind, or a spiritual quagmire. If you are not already giving proper attention to the people and things that are important to you (including yourself), now is the time to change it.

Hopefully, by now, you have concluded that the rewards of victory are not necessarily measured by financial wealth, a big home, fame, or material possessions. There is absolutely nothing wrong with having aspirations of such things, as discussed earlier, but to be whole and complete requires much more. You must understand that these worldly things are temporary, on loan from our creator and you must be balanced by having eternal aspirations as part of your life ledger. Worldly material possessions bring temporary satisfaction and are physically temporary themselves. When we pass from this physical world any material possessions become the property of someone else.

Along these lines, a loving, responsible parent teaches a child to love and serve others as they set the example by living like this themselves, understanding that those teachings and philosophy will be passed on for generations to come. Be a good example to those around you by being consistent in your actions and manners with dignity, pride, and self-respect. Victorious living requires a vision and a desire to leave the world a better place simply as a result of your existence.

Don't be concerned if your platform of influence is limited to a small audience. The key word is "influence". Though tossing a small pebble in a gigantic ocean doesn't appear to have raised the level of the ocean, one can intuitively conclude that the water has risen ever so slightly by the fluid displacement caused by the pebble. So it is with our influence towards others through words and actions. It may appear that our influence is insignificant, much like tossing a pebble into a vast ocean, when in reality, an accumulation of pebbles over time would fill an ocean and change the landscape of the world.

Are you tossing pebbles of influence? If not, begin today, making it a habit and ritual in your daily living to take every opportunity to toss a pebble of influence. You may never see the results but be assured that as you put this into practice, others will be influenced.

Keep in mind that we are not the ones who do the changing. It is not our place or responsibility. We are only responsible for being willing to accept the challenge of being the catalyst for change. We never know the degree of influence that we leave by our way of daily living, whether positive or negative, but we can be assured that our legacy will be either one of positive influence or negative influence and that the landscape of the world will be forever different as a result.

This practice of legacy awareness by having the end result in mind as you go about your daily activities can bring about significant change in your life and the lives of others around you. It may appear that the degree of influence is narrow, but think about the thousands, if not millions of people that will be affected in your lifetime and after your lifetime as a result of right living. Let's say, for example, that you positively influence 10 people in a lifetime, which is very conservative. If those 10 people influence another 10 people, then a simple math equation is 10 X 10 = 100. If this process is carried on through 4 more levels of influence, then you have realistically influenced 1,000,000 people.

There will be those who would scoff at this by using a narrow-minded approach, not understanding that the goal is not a number. The goal should be to use whatever influence you have to effect positive change in your corner of the world, whether it be large or small, ultimately affecting positive change in your life and that of others around you. If everyone would do this one thing, we would live in a utopian world.

As mentioned earlier, success is not measured by what we accomplish; it is measured by what we accomplish based on our abilities. The kid who used 100 percent of their ability to sell 5 boxes of Girl Scout Cookies was more successful than another who sold 100 boxes but had the ability to sell 200 boxes.

Never compare yourself to another when evaluating your performance. The person with whom you are comparing yourself may not have half of the ability you have or they may have twice your ability. In either case, the comparison and, thus, the evaluation is not accurate.

You are in competition with one person. That person's name is YOU. Use whatever influence and ability that you have and you will be victorious.

Be mindful to always celebrate when others are victorious. There is no room for jealousy or envy for those who are victorious. When you have a co-worker, a friend or a family member who gets a win, congratulate them and sincerely be thankful that something good happened for them. People who are genuinely happy to see others succeed most often find success themselves.

Are you living victorious? Are you recognizing and giving thanks for the victories around you? Do you celebrate others who experience victory? If not, begin today to claim victory. There is power in it!! ***Before you can do something, you must be something.*** Be Victorious!

I have an unshakeable Will to survive and to succeed

The attribute of strong will is most often misunderstood. There are those who believe "with willpower I will make anything happen". While this is a valiant and courageous thought, it most certainly is not accurate. Willpower alone will not pave the way for a bountiful life, but it will help get the ground ready for the pavement. It is the bulldozer that pushes obstacles out of the way and smooths the ground for advancement toward a worthy cause that paves the way toward achievement.

A strong will is nothing more than focused determination fueled by a burning desire to accomplish, achieve or attain a particular thing. We all have desires (wants), but until that desire changes to a burning desire, the chances of our desire becoming reality are slim to none. Once a desire (meaningless want) becomes a burning desire (goal with purpose and meaning), the unshakeable will has been unleashed. I have had a desire to write a book for many years. It didn't happen until it became a burning desire and here we are, almost complete. A determined will cleared the way and the words began to flow.

> *"Strength does not come from physical capacity. It comes from an indomitable will." - Mahatma Gandhi*

Obviously, a goal with purpose and meaning must precede the will, thus making true the fact that **Will** alone is not enough. Will without a goal is aimless and pointless, while a goal without the will to achieve is nothing more than want. One without the other is a fruitless endeavor full of disappointment and failure.

The attribute of will is like any other. It can be enhanced through practice and application. Once a worthy cause or goal is identified, pour your soul into its achievement (burning desire) and do whatever it takes within the laws of the universe to see it to the end and then you will have sharpened the attribute of willpower. Know what you want and do whatever it takes, following ethical principles, to get what you want is to have exercised your will upon it.

> *It is fatal to enter any war without the will to win it." - Douglas MacArthur*

Douglas Macarthur knew a thing or two about war as a very successful General in the United States Army. He made a promise to the Philippine people after being ousted from the islands by the Japanese in World War 2 that he would return. He had a goal and a burning desire to see the goal through and he returned as he said he would. He exercised his will to accomplish a worthy cause. Whether it is war or the challenges of everyday life, victory comes to those with the will to win.

Unleash someone with an unshakeable will and something will happen. With your goal in sight, a clear vision of the thing you have decided to do and an unshakable will, complete this sentence: I will _____" (you fill in the blank). When all of your focus and willpower are unleashed, the circumstances that arise are almost always either diminished or destroyed as you move forward toward that which you will be or have.

Set the goal, apply the will and the road to success will flow beneath you. There will surely be potholes, detours and road hazards along the way, but proper application of the will will make the journey toward your destination a smoother ride. The potholes, detours and road hazards are reminders that success is not easy, but as you stay focused, keep your hands on the wheel, keep your eye on the prize, understanding that nothing worthwhile is easy, mile after mile rolls by as you press forward to your destination.

Anyone can choose easily, but you are not just anyone; you were created for much more. Choose for yourself today the will to survive, succeed and strengthen that will each day through daily practice and daily pressing on, which becomes easier and easier. Where there is a will, there is a way.

Before you can do something, you must be something. Do you have an unshakable will to survive and succeed? I do.

I am eXtremely grateful for the precious gift of life

We have so much to be grateful for. We are so blessed. There are those who have, without a doubt, been dealt a bad hand and there are others that, due to circumstances, some unforeseen and some self-inflicted, would dispute their having plenty to be thankful for, but if you are healthy, have a home to live in, food to eat, clothes to wear and people in your life who love you, you are rich!

Oftentimes, we unwittingly spend a tremendous amount of time and energy participating in what I like to call "wishy-washy activities". We wish we had this or we wish we had that when all the while everything we really need is ours. If we consistently direct our focus on wants rather than needs, we tend to focus our attitude on lack rather than plenty. This type of activity not only delivers lack but also washes away our appreciation for the many things that really matter and are already in our possession. This wishy-washy activity steals our joy and drains our energy, yet it becomes a daily activity if we are not careful. As a result, we are pushed farther and farther into the rate race that has no finish line.

If we are not careful, we wish our lives away, day after day, wishing for this or wishing for that. This type of behavior is unhealthy and unproductive. It demands our attention 24-7, steals our joy and drains our energy. Be careful what you ask for; you just might get it.

Have you ever heard the term "the more you get, the more you want"? This simple but profound statement is true in many of our lives. The nice, comfortable home just isn't big enough, new enough, modern enough, rustic enough or perhaps we say to ourselves, "My friends have nicer homes." The dependable automobile just isn't large enough, luxurious enough, fast enough, sporty enough or perhaps we say to ourselves, "My friends have nicer automobiles". It could be that one home is just not enough; we need a secondary residence for recreation. Two homes would be much better, especially if one were a beach home or a mountain retreat home.

We come up with various, sometimes creative, ways to justify our "get more" mentality. "I work hard and I deserve the finer things of this world," we tell ourselves. "If old Moneybags deserves it, then so do I," we convincingly repeat in our mind as we sign on the dotted line on the loan papers. "You only live once, so I may as well live it up" is a justification often used for getting more and more and more.

Finally, one day, we have more, more, more and guess what.......it still isn't enough. Unfortunately, by this time, we are eyeball deep in debt and unable to pull ourselves out of the financial hole we have gotten ourselves into, not to mention the constant worry and demands on our time to take good care of our little empire. The very thing that was sure to bring us joy reminds us of being the parent to a newborn baby. It keeps us up at night and demands our constant attention as we deal with the crap that goes along with it. Staying up at night to take care of a newborn child is one thing, but staying up worried about our little empire is another.

Let's be very clear. There is absolutely nothing wrong with dreaming big. As a matter of fact, I would highly suggest it. There is also nothing wrong with desiring or having possessions and I am certainly not criticizing anyone with a beach home or mountain retreat. If we lived in a world without people with big dreams, we would still be riding horseback from point A to point B and lighting our homes with candles. I much prefer my automobile to get me from point A to point B and I certainly enjoy my all-electric home…… especially thermostatically controlled heat & air!

The whole point of this section is to focus on what we have (fulfillment) rather than what we do not (lack). To accomplish this is very simple. As the old church hymn says, "Count your many blessings; name them one by one". In other words, be grateful for what you have!

> ***"In everything give thanks; for this is God's will for you in Jesus Christ." 1 Thessalonians 5:18***

The practice of gratitude can be a life-changing experience. By simply recognizing the very things that we take for granted yet are necessary to sustain life here on this earth will put you in a different mindset and give you a different perspective. Do yourself a favor. Read the following instructions and perform the exercise:

1. Close your eyes, slowly take a deep breath, briefly hold it, and slowly exhale.
2. Think of the consequences of no air to breathe (If you are not sure what the consequences are, hold your breath as long as you can… disclaimer; the author nor the publisher is responsible for injury as a result of you losing consciousness).
3. Now, be thankful for the air you breathe.

Continue by taking a drink of refreshing cool water. Now, think of the consequences of being on a beautiful tropical island (probably on your wish list) with no source of fresh water and no way of escaping the island (not on your wish list). Now give thanks for the nice refreshing cool water. Take a bite of your favorite food. Think about the millions of people around the world who will not have anything to eat today and be thankful for the food you eat.

Walk through the countryside and admire the beauty of creation as you listen to the breeze rustle through the leaves and hear the birds singing in the distance. During the day, admire the fluffy clouds floating against the beautiful backdrop of blue sky. At night, take a look at the thousands of stars that glitter in the darkness that thousands of humans have admired for thousands of years. If you get a chance, take a peek through a telescope and admire Saturn's rings, Jupiter and its moons, the deep craters of the moon or the crescent of Venus as it disappears over the horizon. Indeed, we have much to be grateful for.

> *"Give yourself a gift of five minutes of contemplation in awe of everything you see around you. Go outside and turn your attention to the many miracles around you. This five-minute-a-day regimen of appreciation and gratitude will help you to focus your life in awe."[13]* **Wayne Dyer**

When we take the time to truly be grateful for the many blessings that we have, our focus is diverted from challenges (things we would rather not have in our lives), which produce an attitude of lack and moves our focus on things that have value to us (things we want in our lives) which promotes an attitude of gain. In other words, an attitude of gratitude provides happiness to the soul.

Obviously, we could continue page after page, identifying overlooked blessings, but hopefully, you get the point. Be grateful for the many blessings you already have!!

---

13   https://www.brainyquote.com/quotes/wayne_dyer_718043?src=t_gratitude

If you want to experience the power of gratitude, get a notebook and begin to list the many things that you have to be grateful for. The most obvious gifts are those special gifts from God, such as family and friends. As you make your list, name each of them on the list. Truly pause and appreciate them for who they are and the significance they play in your life. Think for a moment how you would feel if they were no longer in your life in order to get a real understanding of their value to you and your gratitude for them. Past this, list other things that are not as significant but play a role in your life, especially those that we take for granted. List the things like water, air, food, and even toilet paper (try doing without that one). List anything that comes to mind, no matter how simple. Nothing is trivial on this list. Visit your gratitude list daily, continue to grow the list and focus on how blessed you are for everything on the list. This simple but effective activity will give you an important attitude of gratitude and put emphasis on how truly blessed you are. It is simple, but it is effective to put things in perspective. It helps you focus on what is truly important rather than wasting your time focusing on trivial circumstances that come and go daily.

Another unique way to practice gratitude was shared by my good friend Buddy Gray before he lost his battle with cancer. Buddy would carry a gratitude rock in his pocket. Each time he reached into his pocket and simply touched the gratitude rock, it reminded him to think of something to be grateful for. It is a simple reminder to become consciously aware of the many blessings of life, being grateful for them and naming them one by one.

Buddy and I collected many rocks over the years from various places like Rome, the Mediterranean Ocean, Acadia National Park and yes….beside a country road. The rock from Rome is no more valuable than the rock collected beside a country road, nor does any rock collected hold any magical properties or mystical powers. So, it's just a rock, right? No. It is not just a rock. It is a gratitude rock. It is my reminder of the many blessings of life and there are many!

When you find yourself "down in dumps" read over your gratitude list. Soak in the list as you realize the things on the list are the things in life that are truly important. Understand also that many of the things on your gratitude list are on the "wish list" of many others around the world who are less fortunate than you. **You are blessed!**

When you reach into your pocket for the keys to your vehicle and inadvertently brush against the edge of your gratitude rock, stop whatever you are doing, pause your mind from wherever it is and think of one little thing that you are grateful for. Instantly, you will be reminded that there is much to be thankful for. An attitude of gratitude will change your life! I repeat once more: **You are blessed!**

Perhaps one of the most overlooked activities that many of us are guilty of is not expressing gratitude for the many blessings that we have. It is so easy to overlook the blessings of life and focus on the difficulties of life. Understand this: what you focus on expands, so be careful to focus intentionally on your many blessings.

Many complain and grumble about "having" to show up to work. When they get to work, they complain and grumble about "having" to work instead of focusing on the blessing of having a job. It is always interesting to see a professional athlete dissatisfied with a multimillion-dollar contract offer because it is not enough. The focus is on the paycheck rather than the privilege of being a professional athlete.

This was not the case with the late Pat Tillman. Pat Tillman turned down a multimillion-dollar contract renewal with the Arizona Cardinals to enlist as an Army Ranger after the terrorist attacks of 9/11, ultimately losing his life on the battlefield in Afghanistan. It has to be one of the most unselfish acts in the history of mankind. Pat Tillman could have accepted the multimillion-dollar contract, continued to play the game that he loved to play and enjoyed all of the benefits and notoriety that came along with it, yet he understood the gift of freedom and paid the ultimate price to defend that gift for fellow countryman, as thousands of brave men and women have done and continue to do today. All accounts indicate that Pat Tillman understood the precious gift of life and lived his life to the fullest.

We could all take a page from Pat Tillman's playbook. We should wake up each day with a smile on our faces because we have been gifted with another day of life. Furthermore, focusing on the gift of life rather than the circumstances of life provides a positive perspective, which then provides a positive mental attitude and ultimately generates positive results. If your results are unfavorable as a result of being under the circumstances, get out from under the circumstances and see your life for what it really is: a precious gift.

Be extremely grateful for the precious gift of life. You will be blessed and so will those around you. ***Before you can do something, you must be something***. Are you extremely grateful for this precious gift of life? I am.

I am Young at heart

Why is it that once we reach a certain age, we consider ourselves as old? For some people, that age is 40, for some 50, for some 60 and yes, there are those that still consider themselves young at age 100+.

It is a fact that as we age, our mind tells us one thing while our body tells us something else. I can remember, at age 30, wondering why anyone would ever quit participating in athletic events. As a matter of fact, I can remember making the statement that I would never do that. With three Achilles surgeries later, along with other things that go along with an additional 25+ years of age, my perspective about participating in athletic events has changed,,… **BUT…**, I am still young at heart.

Although there are many things that I can no longer physically do, I do not consider myself old. As a matter of fact, I am still young! So why would I still feel young? Attitude of mind. Though my body has a little more mileage, my attitude of mind has not changed from the days of my youth in perspective of age. I still see myself as young, so therefore I am young.

How you see yourself is so important. It will affect the way you live, look and perform as a person. I might add that it will also affect those around you, so be very careful that you continue to see and believe yourself to be young. It will add years to your life and give those around you a more enjoyable experience.

There are many people who have influenced my attitude of considering myself young, my mother being one of them. As I am writing this, Kathy, my two sisters and I are planning a 90th birthday party for my beloved mother, who still drives to most places she wants to go, stays busy spending time with family and friends and as she puts it, still visits the "old folks" who can't get out and about.

Aside from good genetics, her attitude of remaining young has played a great role in her ability to remain active. Most people who see her and are aware of her active lifestyle cannot believe she is 70, much less pushing 90.

She has never allowed age to hold her back from the things she wanted to do. She earned a college degree at age 43, a Master's degree at age 45 and spent 22 years as a teacher. As a result, she has traveled the world, enjoyed a fruitful retirement and still enjoys hearing from former students and co-workers whose lives were positively affected because she didn't let age prevent her from living her dream of earning a college degree and having a career as a teacher. Kudos to you, Mimi. Stay young.

My mother could have easily "kicked back" after raising three kids. At that stage in her life, my father was very successful and provided a good income for the family. We had moved from the two-bedroom one bath home, heated with a coal stove to a modern three bedroom, 2 bath home with electric heat and air conditioning. My sister and I thought we had died and gone to heaven. Instead of standing beside the coal stove to stay warm, we could now sit beside the fireplace in our new home, not because we were cold, but because we wanted to.

Instead of taking it easy, my mother fulfilled her ambition to become the first person in the family to earn a college degree. Kudos to my father, too.

He was very generous in helping make her dream become a reality with moral support and financial assistance. One of my favorite stories about her journey was how my father would sell a few cows when it came time to pay her tuition. He loved his cows but was willing to see them go to make my mother's dream of a college degree a reality.

Her decision to remain young at heart had a lasting effect on her children. When it came time to graduate from high school, there was no question about whether we would go to college, only where we would go to college. My two sisters graduated with degrees in education from the University of Montevallo, and I graduated with a business degree from the University of Alabama. I later earned a Master of Business Administration from Samford University. I truly believe that none of this would have happened if it were not for my father's generosity and my mother's ambition despite being 43 years young.

Being young at heart has served my mother well, and it will serve you well, too. Her attitude toward youth has given me the perspective to keep moving toward accomplishing things I always wanted to do.

At a very early age, my mother took my youngest sister and I to a concert at the local high school. I couldn't tell you the name of the group or even what kind of music they played but I can tell you that I was mesmerized by the drums. From that very moment, I wanted to be a drummer; however, my mother wanted me to be a pianist.

My sister went on to become a very accomplished pianist, but my experience at the piano was a flop. We had the same teacher who taught the same thing, but I didn't make it. I didn't make it because I wanted to be a drummer.

Years went by and at age 40, I decided I wanted to learn how to play guitar. While my wife was away for the weekend, I purchased an electric guitar and amplifier from a local pawn shop. I played the guitar so much that weekend that my fingers were raw. Week after week, I would play the guitar in my spare time until I taught myself how to play guitar.

After I learned guitar, I decided it was time to fulfill my dream of being a drummer. I pulled the sheets that covered the old drum kit I had purchased from someone needing money years earlier and began to torment my family as I taught myself to play the drums in the basement of our home.

My big breakthrough came one day on the way to church. Our interim music director, who heard it from a friend who heard it from a friend that I could play drums, called my cell phone and asked me to play drums for our Sunday morning service since our drummer was not going to make it.

As I remember it, my debut as a drummer was a disaster. I was so nervous that the sticks flew from my hands on more than one occasion and quite frankly, it was terrible. Here I was, 40-something and finally doing something I had always wanted to do and had blown it.

Much to my amazement, the next time the drummer was not able to make it, I was asked to play. I am convinced that it wasn't because I was good enough to do it; it was because there was no one else to fill in. Whatever the reason, I overcame my fears, let my heart take over and played.

Since then, I have occasionally played Bass guitar, guitar and still enjoy drumming. If I am in town on weekends I enjoy serving as drummer for our church orchestra. While I am far from being a professional musician, I enjoy doing something that I have dreamed of doing for years and hopefully fulfilling a small part of the purpose for which I was created to fulfill.

There are so many reasons why none of this should ever have happened. A terrible debut, a fear of failure, and certainly waiting such a long time to begin. Any of these excuses could have kept me from doing what I love to do.

I am sure that you, too, have something in mind you have dreamed of doing, something you were perhaps created to do, purposely and intentionally. Whatever it is, begin right now and just do it. While it is never too late, there is no time like the present to start. Go to the pawn shop and pick up a guitar, pull the covers from the drum kit in the basement, enroll in a college course, whatever it is, and never let anything, especially age, deter you from accomplishing the dream that you have.

Before you can do something, you must be something. Are you young at heart? I am and I am not finished yet!

I live life with Zeal

What a way to wrap up the ABCs of Transformation......Zeal. To live life with Zeal simply means to put a little pizazz into life. According to SIRI, it means showing great energy or enthusiasm in pursuit of a cause or objective. SIRI isn't always accurate, but in this case, SIRI is right. I would add that in your case, make sure the cause or objective is worthy.

A worthy cause or objective is one that really lights your fire. It is a cause or objective that not only serves you but serves others. It is precise but selfless. It is challenging but obtainable. It is something that, once accomplished, leaves the world a better place.

Very simply put, life is short so live it to the fullest. Live life in a way that when you get to the end of the road, there is no gas left in the tank and you can look back on a life of accomplishment, accomplishment that brought you and those around you joy while making the world a better place.

Begin early with your bucket list. Live life in a way that you are constantly filling the bucket up and draining it by experiencing things that you want to experience in your lifetime while being responsible to yourself and others physically, mentally and spiritually. As long as it doesn't interfere with your physical, mental or spiritual well-being or that of others and it is something within financial reason……..DO IT NOW, if possible.

Sometimes, there are obstacles such as finances, physical abilities, or mental abilities that make our bucket list of dreams seem unreachable, but there is something about setting our sights on something big and setting out with zeal in pursuit of those things. When we pursue big dreams, even if we do not accomplish them, something good happens. Sometimes, we find that the energy and enthusiasm that we have expended toward our objective has left us short of where we intended but in a much better place. Sometimes, we find ourselves in a totally different place than we intended, and the light bulb goes off in our head to tell us that we are exactly where we should be as a result of our pursuit. Sometimes, we reach the mountaintop that we set out to conquer, and we see the vastness before us, realizing that we have only begun to accomplish that for which we were created. In every case, we moved forward toward the destination that we ourselves put in our personal GPS.

The pursuit that began with a destination in mind, a road map to that destination and an attitude of zeal has opened our eyes to limitless possibilities. Even the unexpected detours serve to enlighten and provide opportunities for personal growth, building character along the way. The detours may slow you down, but the climb is still before you. When the detours come, there is still the mountain to climb, so reenergize the zeal in your heart and climb, climb some more and then climb. No mountain is too tall. Climb with Zeal.

Nothing worth accomplishing is ever easy. It takes sometimes endless hours of study and effort to move just one step up the mountain. Sometimes, we slip and fall on the journey, but when you look back, don't focus on the slips and falls; focus on the progress you have made, climb. When it seems like you cannot take another step, dig deep to find that little part of zeal that still exists and climb.

I believe one of the saddest things would be getting to the end of the road with regrets by not experiencing life to the fullest, knowing that there were many things you wanted to do or intended to do or things you wanted to say that will never be done or said. Live life with zeal so that those things do not get undone or those words are never unspoken.

When there is someone who needs to know that you love them, tell them or better yet, show them by serving them in some way or another that will bring joy to their soul. Brighten up their day with a simple smile or a hug. It is amazing what happens when we are able to brighten someone's day. A selfless act of service that brings happiness to another person's heart not only brightens their day but also brightens ours.

To live a zealous life means to live big, not in a "showy" kind of way but an impactful kind of way. Living big means influencing others in a positive way, not for your glory but for their benefit. When we live big, others around us live big. We are lifted up by lifting up others around us. If we do this selflessly, the blessings to ourselves and those around us are immeasurable.

Les Brown[14] says we should not choose to die with the music still in us. The cemetery is the richest piece of real estate on the planet because there is a song in the cemetery that was never written, recorded, or performed. In the cemetery, there is a book never written, published, or read. In the cemetery, there is the idea that would have changed the world as we know it. The song, the book and the idea lay forever dormant because the person died with the music still in them.

Let your music play every day of your life. Leave nothing on the table. ***Before you can do something, you must be something.*** I live life with Zeal. Do you?

---

14   https://www.azquotes.com/author/2022-Les_Brown

Conclusion

I hope that you have enjoyed reading this book and I truly hope that you have been able to take something away from the ideas discussed that will help you be successful at whatever endeavor you undertake but mainly, live a successful life and leave this world a better place than you found it.

The main thing to understand about yourself is that you can become anything that you choose to become by choosing for yourself the attributes that you believe make you who you want to be and leave a significant mark on your part of the world. You are truly a special creation, and you were created for purpose. Out of the millions of people who have been created, you are a special and unique spirit with specific gifts and talents. As you discover and expand these gifts one by one and as you begin to share your talents with the world, you find significance. Always remember that you indeed are a child of God and your living small does not serve the world.

Be the person that you were designed to be by intentionally developing and applying the ABCs of Transformation. Intention is a powerful tool that is in your grasp. Be aware of it and use it to serve yourself and others around you. Intentionally be the masterpiece that was sculpted at the hand of God.

What started as a project to provide written instruction to my children, a manual of how to manifest into their lives the enriching things of this life and how best to make themselves, those around them and this world a better place through intentional thoughts and actions turned into something totally unexpected. I had no idea what this process would reveal in my life. As I researched, studied, learned, observed people and experienced many things, I learned a lot about myself.

I learned that I had a long way to go to becoming the person that I so desired, the person described on the pages of this book. I learned that the journey to the destination I desired, the person I wanted to be, was long and difficult. I also learned that there is no true destination or finish line. Yes, I will pass from this world, but my soul will journey on, for I am not a physical being; I am a spiritual being having a physical experience. While on Earth, there is always another mountain to climb, another valley to traverse or another river to cross as I journey through life. There are slips and stumbles along the way, setbacks and obstacles that serve to prompt me to wave the white flag of surrender or push forward. There are circumstances that arise that will either make me bitter or make me better.

I have learned that sometimes I may wave the white flag or allow my thoughts to wander toward bitterness as I choose to live "under the circumstances." I have also learned that I can do a good job of disappointing myself and those around me. Sometimes, I can really make a mess of things. I have learned all these things, but most importantly, I have learned that I always bounce back when I make my mind up to do so through exercising proper thought and intentionally doing the things and thinking the thoughts that get me back on track. I have also learned to forgive myself for failing and extend that grace to others who are not so kind-hearted in their actions towards me.

That is the true testament of love when we can rise above the feelings of disappointment in ourselves or others and choose to love ourselves and others enough to forgive. As you move forward through disappointments in yourself or others, choose the power of forgiveness and love.

As you move toward the pinnacle that you intentionally choose for yourself, be certain of this: ***life is what you make it***. You can climb as high as you decide to climb, go as far as you decide to go and then some. It is up to you to choose your altitude and your distance, so never forget that ***you must be something before you can do something***! Happy journey to you!

Kendall Williams, MBA

Kendall Williams' upbringing on a farm in central Alabama instilled in him the values of hard work, discipline, and resourcefulness, shaping his journey across various facets of life. His academic path led him from the University of Alabama, where he obtained a degree in business, to Sanford University for his MBA, laying the groundwork for a diverse and successful career in business. Kendall's professional experience spans manufacturing, sales, and insurance within the public sector, earning him numerous accolades for his achievements and service. His entrepreneurial spirit has seen him co-own a multimillion-dollar manufacturing enterprise, a real estate venture, and most recently, take the helm of his family's farm, managing these diverse responsibilities simultaneously.

Transforming from a natural introvert to an extroverted individual, Kendall has harnessed the strengths of both personality types to foster significant personal growth. He values this transformation above his business successes, viewing personal development as an ongoing journey without a definitive end. Kendall believes in the importance of daily progress for the benefit of self and others, embracing challenges as opportunities for improvement.

Despite a busy schedule, Kendall prioritizes reading, studying, and writing, alongside his commitments to faith, family, and professional development. His real-life experiences and practical way of thinking make his writing easy to understand and relatable to real life. Kendall loves being able to serve others by sharing his experiences and his passion for personal improvement. He cherishes the time spent with family and friends on the family farm, where the slower pace of life allows him to reflect, plan, and free his mind as he moves toward the next chapter of personal improvement.

Kendall can be contacted at: www.theabcsoftransformation.com

www.ingramcontent.com/pod-product-compliance
Lightning Source LLC
Chambersburg PA
CBHW050633160426
43194CB00010B/1653